The Lectionary
2006

First published in Great Britain in 2005

Society for Promoting Christian Knowledge
36 Causton Street
London SW1P 4ST

British Library Cataloguing-in-Publication Data
A catalogue record for this book is available from the British Library

ISBN 0-281-05751-6

1 3 5 7 9 10 8 6 4 2

Typeset by Land & Unwin (Data Sciences) Ltd, Northamptonshire
Printed in Great Britain by Bath Press Ltd, Bath

CONTENTS

UNDERSTANDING THE

Column 3 (Common Worship)
On Principal Feasts, Principal Holy Days, Sundays and Festivals this gives the Principal Service Lectionary, intended for use at the main service of the day (in most churches the mid-morning service), whether or not it is a Eucharist.

On other weekdays this gives the Daily Eucharistic Lectionary for those wanting a semi-continuous pattern of readings and a psalm for Holy Communion. It is most useful in a church where there is a daily celebration and a core community that worships together day by day, though its use is not restricted to that.

Column 4 (Common Worship)
On Principal Feasts, Principal Holy Days, Sundays and Festivals this gives the Third Service Lectionary. Many churches will have no need of it, for it comes into use only if the Principal and Second Service Lectionaries have been used. Its most likely use is at Morning Prayer (when this is not the Principal Service). Where psalms are recommended for use in the morning, these also appear in this column.

On other weekdays this provides the psalmody and readings for Morning Prayer. Where two or more psalms are appointed, the psalm in bold italic may be used as the only psalm. Psalms printed in round brackets ( ) may be omitted if they are used as an opening canticle at Morning Prayer. Where † is printed after the psalm number, the psalm may be shortened if desired. For those wishing to follow the Ordinary Time psalm cycle throughout the year (except for the period between 19 December and the Epiphany and from the Monday of Holy Week to the Saturday of Easter Week), this is printed as an alternative to the seasonal provision.

Column 1
The date

COMMON WORSHIP

October 2006

Sunday Principal Service
Weekday Eucharist

Third Service
Morning Prayer

►14 Sa

Gal. 3. 22–end
Ps. 105. 1–7
Luke 11. 27–28

►Ps. *76*; 79
2 Kings 4. 1–37
Acts 25. 13–end

15 G S

THE EIGHTEENTH SUNDAY AFTER TRINITY (Proper 23)
Track 1   *Track 2*
Job 23. 1–9, 16–end   Amos 5. 6–7, 10–15
►Ps. 22. 1–15   Ps. 90. 12–end
Heb. 4. 12–end   Heb. 4. 12–end
Mark 10. 17–31   Mark 10. 17–31

Ps. 129; 130
Isa. 50. 4–10
Luke 13. 22–30

16 G M

Nicholas Ridley, Bishop of London, and Hugh Latimer, Bishop of Worcester, Reformation Martyrs, 1555
Gal. 4. 21–24, 26–27, 31; 5. 1   Ps. *80*; 82
Ps. 113   2 Kings ch. 5
Luke 11. 29–32   Acts 26. 1–23

DEL 28

G

Week number of Daily Eucharistic Lectionary

Column 2 provides for Common Worship:
- the name of the Principal Holy Day, Sunday, Festival or Lesser Festival;
- a note of other Commemorations for mention in prayers;
- any general note that applies to the whole *Common Worship* provision for the day;
- one of the options where there are two options for readings at the Eucharist or Principal Service;
- an indication of the liturgical colour.

Readings: Readings occur in this column only in two circumstances. On Sundays after Trinity where there are two 'tracks' for the Principal Service readings (where there is a choice of first reading and psalm, but the second reading and Gospel are the same in both tracks), Track 1 appears in this column. On Lesser Festivals throughout the year, where there are readings for that festival that are alternative to the semi-continuous Daily Eucharistic Lectionary, these also appear in this column.

Colour: An upper-case letter indicates the liturgical colour of the day. A lower-case second colour indicates the colour for a Lesser Festival while the upper-case letter indicates the continuing seasonal colour.

LECTIONARY

Column 5 (Common Worship)
On Principal Feasts, Principal Holy Days, Sundays and Festivals this gives the Second Service Lectionary, intended for use when a second set of readings is required. Its most likely use is in the evening, when the Principal Service Lectionary has been used in the morning. Sometimes it might be used at an evening Eucharist. Where the second reading is not a Gospel reading, an alternative to meet this need is provided. Where psalms are recommended for use in the evening, these also appear in this column.
On other weekdays this provides the psalmody and readings for Evening Prayer. Where two or more psalms are provided, the psalm in bold italic may be used as the only psalm. Psalms printed in round brackets ( ) may be omitted if they are used as an opening canticle at Evening Prayer. Where † is printed after the psalm number, the psalm may be shortened if desired. For those wishing to follow the Ordinary Time psalm cycle throughout the year (except for the period between 19 December and the Epiphany and from the Monday of Holy Week to the Saturday of Easter Week), this is printed as an alternative to the seasonal provision.

Column 7 (Book of Common Prayer)
This provides the readings for Morning Prayer, together with psalm provision where it varies from the BCP monthly cycle.

A letter to indicate liturgical colour in this column indicates a change of colour before Evening Prayer. The symbol in bold lower case, ct, indicates that the Collect at Evening Prayer should be that of the following day.

BOOK OF COMMON PRAYER

Second Service Evening Prayer	Calendar and Holy Communion	Morning Prayer	Evening Prayer
Ps. 81; 84 Ecclus 15. 11–end or Ezek. 14 1–11 Mark 14. 66–end **ct**	G	2 Kings 4. 1–37 Acts 25. 13–end	Ecclus. 15. 11–end or Ezek. 14. 1–11 Mark 14. 66–end **ct**
THE EIGHTEENTH SUNDAY AFTER TRINITY			
Ps. 127 [128] Josh. 5.13 – 6.20 Matt. 11. 20–end	Deut. 6. 4–9 Ps. 122 1 Cor. 1. 4–8 Matt. 22. 34–end G	Ps. 129; 130 Isa. 50. 4–10 Luke 13. 22–30	Ps. 127; [128] Josh. 5.13 – 6.20 Matt. 11. 20–end
Ps. 85; 86 Ecclus. 16. 17–end or Ezek. 14. 12–end Mark 15. 1–15	G	2 Kings ch. 5 Acts 26. 1–23	Ecclus. 16. 17–end or Ezek. 14. 12–end Mark 15. 1–15

A letter to indicate liturgical colour in this column indicates a change of colour before Evening Prayer. The symbol in bold lower case, ct, indicates that the Collect at Evening Prayer should be that of the following day.

Column 6 provides for Book of Common Prayer:
• the name of the Principal Holy Day, Sunday, Festival or Lesser Festival;
• any general note that applies to the whole Prayer Book provision for the day and an indication of points at which users may wish to draw on Common Worship material on the opposite page where the BCP has no provision;
• the lectionary for the Eucharist on any day for which provision is made;
• an indication of liturgical colour (see column 2).

Column 8 (Book of Common Prayer)
This provides the readings for Evening Prayer, together with psalm provision where it varies from the BCP monthly cycle.

Making Choices in *Common Worship*

Common Worship makes provision for a variety of pastoral and liturgical circumstances. It needs to, for it has to serve some church communities where Morning Prayer, Holy Communion and Evening Prayer are all celebrated every day, and yet be useful also in a church with only one service a week, and that service varying in form and time from week to week.

At the beginning of the year, some decisions in principle need to be taken.

In relation to the Calendar, a decision needs to be taken whether to keep The Epiphany on Friday 6 January or on Sunday 8 January, the Presentation of Christ (Candlemas) on Thursday 2 February or on Sunday 29 January, and whether to keep the Feast of All Saints on Wednesday 1 November or on Sunday 5 November.

In relation to the Lectionary, the initial choices every year to decide in relation to Sundays are:

- which of the services on a Principal Feast, Principal Holy Day, Sunday or Festival constitutes the 'Principal Service'; then use the Principal Service Lectionary (column 3) consistently for that service through the year;
- during the Sundays after Trinity, whether to use Track 1 of the Principal Service Lectionary (column 2), where the first reading stays over several weeks with one Old Testament book read semi-continuously, or Track 2 (column 3), where the first reading is chosen for its relationship to the Gospel reading of the day;
- which, if any, service on a Principal Feast, Principal Holy Day, Sunday or Festival constitutes the 'Second Service'; then use the Second Service Lectionary (column 5) consistently for that service through the year;
- which if any, service on a Principal Feast, Principal Holy Day, Sunday or Festival constitutes the 'Third Service'; then use the Third Service Lectionary (column 4) consistently for that service through the year.

And in relation to weekdays:

- whether to use the Daily Eucharistic Lectionary (column 3) consistently for weekday celebrations of Holy Communion (with the exception of Principal Feasts, Principal Holy Days and Festivals) or to make some use of the Lesser Festival provision;
- whether to follow the first psalm provision in column 4 (morning) and column 5 (evening), where psalms during the seasons have a seasonal flavour but in ordinary time follow a sequential pattern; or to follow the alternative provision in the same columns, where psalms follow the sequential pattern throughout the year, except for the period between 19 December and The Epiphany and from the Monday of Holy Week to the Saturday of Easter Week; or to follow the psalm cycle in the Book of Common Prayer, where they are nearly always used 'in course'.

The flexibility of *Common Worship* is intended to enable the church and the minister to find the most helpful provision for them. But once a decision is made, it is advisable to stay with that decision through the year or at the very least through a complete season.

Book of Common Prayer

A separate Lectionary for the Book of Common Prayer is no longer issued. Provision is made on the right-hand pages of this Lectionary for BCP worship on all Sundays in the year, for the major festivals and for Morning and Evening Prayer. The Epistles and Gospels for Holy Communion are those of 1662, with the additions and variations of 1928, now authorized under the *Common Worship* overall provision. The Old Testament readings and psalms for these services, formerly appended to the Series One Holy Communion service, may be used but are not mandatory with the 1662 order.

Readings for Morning and Evening Prayer, which are the same as those for *Common Worship*, are set out in the BCP section for Sundays and weekdays. The special psalm provision of the BCP is given. Otherwise the Psalter is read in course daily through each month.

The Calendar observes BCP dates when these differ from those of *Common Worship*, for example, St Thomas on 21 December. Additional commemorations in the *Common Worship* Calendar are not included, but those who wish to observe them may use the *Collects and Post Communions in Traditional Language: Lesser Festivals, Common of the Saints, Special Occasions* (Church House Publishing).

The Lectionaries of 1871 and 1922, to be found in many copies of the BCP, are still authorized and may be used, but (with the exception of the psalms and readings for Holy Communion mentioned above) the Additional Alternative Lectionary (1961) is no longer authorized for public worship.

Although those who use the BCP, for private or public worship or both, are free to follow any of the authorized lectionaries, there is much to be said for common usage across the Church of England, so that the same passages are being read by all. It is of course appropriate that BCP readings should be taken from the Authorized or King James Version for harmony of style, with the daily recitation of the BCP Psalter.

The integrity of the BCP as the traditional source of worship in the Church of England is not in any way affected by the use of a common lectionary for the daily offices.

CERTAIN DAYS AND OCCASIONS COMMONLY OBSERVED

Plough Sunday may be observed on 8 January 2006.

The Week of Prayer for Christian Unity may be observed from 18 to 25 January 2006.

Education Sunday may be observed on 12 February 2006.

Rogation Sunday may be observed on 21 May 2006.

The Feast of Dedication is observed on the anniversary of the dedication or consecration of a church, or, when the actual date is unknown, on 1 October 2006. In CW 29 October 2006 is an alternative date.

Ember Days. CW encourages the bishop to set the Ember Days in each diocese in the week before the ordinations whereas in BCP the dates are fixed.

Days of Discipline and Self-Denial in CW are the weekdays of Lent and all Fridays in the year, except all Principal Feasts and Festivals outside Lent and Fridays between Easter Day and Pentecost. The eves of Principal Feasts are also appropriately kept as days of discipline and self-denial in preparation for the feast.

Days of Fasting and Abstinence according to the BCP are the forty days of Lent, the Ember Days at the four seasons, the three Rogation Days, and all Fridays in the year except Christmas Day. The BCP also orders the observance of the Evens or Vigils before The Nativity of our Lord, The Purification of the Blessed Virgin Mary, The Annunciation of the Blessed Virgin Mary, Easter Day, Ascension Day, Pentecost, and before the following saints' days: Matthias, John the Baptist, Peter, James, Bartholomew, Matthew, Simon and Jude, Andrew, Thomas, and All Saints. (If any of these days falls on Monday, the Vigil is to be kept on the previous Saturday.)

KEY TO LITURGICAL COLOURS

Common Worship suggests appropriate liturgical colours. They are not mandatory and traditional or local use may be followed.

For a detailed discussion of when colours may be used see *Common Worship: Services and Prayers for the Church of England* (Church House Publishing), *New Handbook of Pastoral Liturgy* (SPCK) or *A Companion to Common Worship: Volume 1* (SPCK).

W	White
₩	Gold or white
R	Red
P	Purple (may vary from 'Roman purple' to violet, with blue as an alternative; a Lent array of sackcloth may be used in Lent, and rose pink on The Third Sunday of Advent and Fourth Sunday of Lent.
G	Green

When a lower-case letter accompanies an upper-case letter, the lower-case letter indicates the liturgical colour appropriate to the Lesser Festival of that day, while the upper-case letter indicates the continuing seasonal colour.

PRINCIPAL FEASTS, HOLY DAYS AND FESTIVALS

Principal Feasts, and other principal Holy Days (Ash Wednesday, Maundy Thursday, Good Friday), are printed in **LARGE BOLD CAPITALS** in the Lectionary.

The Epiphany may, for pastoral reasons, be celebrated on The Second Sunday of Christmas. All Saints' Day is celebrated on either 1 November or the Sunday between 30 October and 5 November.

There are no longer proper readings relating to the Holy Spirit on the six days after Pentecost. Instead they have been located on the nine days before Pentecost.

When Patronal and Dedication Festivals are kept as Principal Feasts, they may be transferred to the nearest Sunday, unless that day is already either a Principal Feast or The First Sunday of Advent, The Baptism of Christ, The First Sunday of Lent or Palm Sunday.

Festivals are printed in the Lectionary in SMALL BOLD CAPITALS.

For each day there is a full liturgical provision for the Holy Communion and for Morning and Evening Prayer. Most holy days that are in the category 'Festival' are provided with an optional First Evening Prayer. Its use is entirely at the discretion of the minister. Where it is used, the liturgical colour for the next day should be used at that First Evening Prayer and this has been indicated in the provision on the following pages.

LESSER FESTIVALS AND COMMEMORATIONS

Lesser Festivals (printed in **bold roman** typeface) are observed at the level appropriate to a particular church. The readings and psalms for The Common of the Saints are listed on pages 9–10. In addition, there are special readings appropriate to the Festival listed in the first column. The daily psalms and readings at Morning and Evening Prayer are not usually superseded by those for Lesser Festivals, but the readings and psalms for Holy Communion may on occasion be used at Morning or Evening Prayer.

Commemorations are printed in the Lectionary in *italic* typeface. They do not have collect, psalm or readings, but may be observed by mention in prayers of intercession and thanksgiving. For local reasons, or where there is an established tradition in the wider Church, they may be kept as Lesser Festivals using the appropriate material from The Common of the Saints. Equally, it may be desirable to observe some Lesser Festivals as Commemorations.

If a Lesser Festival or a Commemoration falls on a Principal Feast, Principal Holy Day, Sunday or Festival, it is not normally observed that year, although it may be celebrated, where there is sufficient reason, on the nearest available day. Lesser Festivals and Commemorations which, for this reason, would not be celebrated in 2005–06 are listed on pages 9–10, so that, if desired, they may be mentioned in prayer of intercession and thanksgiving.

LESSER FESTIVALS AND COMMEMORATIONS NOT OBSERVED IN 2005-06

The Lesser Festivals and Commemorations (shown in italics) listed below fall on a Sunday or during Holy Week or Easter Week this year, and are thus not observed in this lectionary.

Common Worship

2005

December

4   *John of Damascus, Monk, Teacher,* c. 749
         Nicholas Ferrar, Deacon, Founder of the Little Gidding Community, 1637

2006

January

22   *Vincent of Saragossa, Deacon, first Martyr of Spain, 304*

March

1   David, Bishop of Menevia, Patron of Wales, c. 601
20   Cuthbert, Bishop of Lindisfarne, Missionary, 687
26   *Harriet Monsell, Founder of the Community of St John the Baptist, Clewer, 1883*

April

9   *Dietrich Bonhoeffer, Lutheran Pastor, Martyr, 1945*
10   William Law, Priest, Spiritual Writer, 1761
         William of Ockham, Friar, Philosopher, Teacher, 1347
11   *George Augustus Selwyn, first Bishop of New Zealand, 1878*
16   *Isabella Gilmore, Deaconess, 1923*
19   Alphege, Archbishop of Canterbury, Martyr, 1012
21   Anselm, Abbot of Le Bec, Archbishop of Canterbury, Teacher, 1109
24   *Mellitus, Bishop of London, first Bishop at St Paul's, 624*
30   *Pandita Mary Ramabai, Translator of the Scriptures, 1922*

May

21   *Helena, Protector of the Holy Places, 330*
25   The Venerable Bede, Monk at Jarrow, Scholar, Historian, 735
         Aldhelm, Bishop of Sherborne, 709
28   *Lanfranc, Prior of Le Bec, Archbishop of Canterbury, Scholar, 1089*

June

4   *Petroc, Abbot of Padstow, 6th century*
18   *Bernard Mizeki, Apostle of the MaShona, Martyr, 1896*

July

16   *Osmund, Bishop of Salisbury, 1099*
23   *Bridget of Sweden, Abbess of Vadstena, 1373*
30   William Wilberforce, Social Reformer, 1833

August

13   Jeremy Taylor, Bishop of Down and Connor, Teacher, 1667
         Florence Nightingale, Nurse, Social Reformer, 1910
         Octavia Hill, Social Reformer, 1912

20	Bernard, Abbot of Clairvaux, Teacher, 1153
	William and Catherine Booth, Founders of the Salvation Army, 1912 and 1890
27	Monica, Mother of Augustine of Hippo, 387

September
3	Gregory the Great, Bishop of Rome, Teacher, 604
17	Hildegard, Abbess of Bingen, Visionary, 1179

October
1	*Remigius, Bishop of Rheims, Apostle of the Franks, 533*
	Anthony Ashley Cooper, Earl of Shaftesbury, Social Reformer, 1885
15	Teresa of Avila, Teacher, 1582
29	James Hannington, Bishop of Eastern Equatorial Africa, Martyr in Uganda, 1885

November
19	Hilda, Abbess of Whitby, 680
	Mechtild, Béguine of Magdeburg, 1280

December
3	*Francis Xavier, Missionary, Apostle of the Indies, 1552*
17	*Eglantine Jebb, Social Reformer, Founder of 'Save the Children', 1928*

Book of Common Prayer
2006

January
8	Lucian, Priest and Martyr, 290
22	Vincent of Saragossa, Deacon, first Martyr of Spain, 304

February
5	Agatha, Martyr in Sicily, 251

March
1	David, Bishop of Menevia, Patron of Wales, *c.* 601
12	Gregory the Great, Bishop of Rome, 604

April
19	Alphege, Archbishop of Canterbury, Martyr, 1012

June
5	Boniface (Wynfrith) of Crediton, Bishop, Apostle of Germany, Martyr, 754

July
2	The Visitation of the Blessed Virgin Mary

September
17	Lambert, Bishop of Maastricht, Martyr, 709

October
1	Remigius, Bishop of Rheims, Apostle of the Franks, 533

December
31	Silvester, Bishop of Rome, 335

THE COMMON OF THE SAINTS

The Blessed Virgin Mary

Genesis 3. 8–15, 20; Isaiah 7. 10–14; Micah 5. 1–4
Acts 1. 12–14; Romans 8. 18–30; Galatians 4. 4–7
Psalms 45. 10–17; 113; 131
Luke 1. 26–38; Luke 1. 39–47; John 19. 25–27

Martyrs

2 Chronicles 24. 17–21; Isaiah 43. 1–7; Jeremiah 11. 18–20; Wisdom 4. 10–15
Romans 8. 35–39; 2 Corinthians 4. 7–15; 2 Timothy 2. 3–7 [8–13]; Hebrews 11. 32–40; 1 Peter 4. 12–19; Revelation 12. 10–12a
Psalms 3; 11; 31. 1–5; 44. 19–24; 126
Matthew 10. 16–22; Matthew 10. 28–39; Matthew 16. 24–26; John 12. 24–26; John 15. 18–21

Teachers of the Faith and Spiritual Writers

1 Kings 3. [6–10] 11–14; Proverbs 4. 1–9; Wisdom 7. 7–10, 15–16; Ecclesiasticus 39. 1–10
1 Corinthians 1. 18–25; 1 Corinthians 2. 1–10; 1 Corinthians 2. 9–16;
Ephesians 3. 8–12; 2 Timothy 4. 1–8; Titus 2. 1–8
Psalms 19. 7–10; 34. 11–17; 37. 30–35; 119. 89–96; 119. 97–104
Matthew 5. 13–19; Matthew 13. 52–58; Matthew 23. 8–12; Mark 4. 1–9; John 16. 12–15

Bishops and Other Pastors

1 Samuel 16. 1, 6–13; Isaiah 6. 1–8; Jeremiah 1. 4–10; Ezekiel 3. 16–21; Malachi 2. 5–7
Acts 20. 28–35; 1 Corinthians 4. 1–5; 2 Corinthians 4. 1–10 (or 1, 2, 5–7); 2 Corinthians 5. 14–20;
1 Peter 5. 1–4
Psalms 1; 15; 16. 5–11; 96; 110
Matthew 11. 25–30; Matthew 24. 42–46; John 10. 11–16; John 15. 9–17; John 21. 15–17

Members of Religious Communities

1 Kings 19. 9–18; Proverbs 10. 27–32; Song of Solomon 8. 6–7; Isaiah 61.10 – 62.5; Hosea 2. 14–15, 19–20
Acts 4. 32–35; 2 Corinthians 10.17 – 11.2; Philippians 3. 7–14; 1 John 2. 15–17; Revelation 19. 1, 5–9
Psalms 34. 1–8; 112. 1–9; 119. 57–64; 123; 131
Matthew 11. 25–30; Matthew 19. 3–12; Matthew 19. 23–30; Luke 9. 57–62; Luke 12. 32–37

Missionaries

Isaiah 52. 7–10; Isaiah 61. 1–3a; Ezekiel 34. 11–16; Jonah 3. 1–5
Acts 2. 14, 22–36; Acts 13. 46–49; Acts 16. 6–10; Acts 26. 19–23; Romans 15. 17–21; 2 Corinthians 5.11 – 6.2
Psalms 67; 87; 97; 100; 117
Matthew 9. 35–38; Matthew 28. 16–20; Mark 16. 15–20; Luke 5. 1–11; Luke 10. 1–9

Any Saint

Genesis 12. 1–4; Proverbs 8. 1–11; Micah 6. 6–8; Ecclesiasticus 2. 7–13 [14–17]
Ephesians 3. 14–19; Ephesians 6. 11–18; Hebrews 13. 7–8, 15–16; James 2. 14–17; 1 John 4. 7–16; Revelation 21. [1–4] 5–7
Psalms 32; 33. 1–5; 119. 1–8; 139. 1–4 [5–12]; 145. 8–14
Matthew 19. 16–21; Matthew 25. 1–13; Matthew 25. 14–30; John 15. 1–8; John 17. 20–26

SPECIAL OCCASIONS
The Guidance of the Holy Spirit
Proverbs 24. 3–7; Isaiah 30. 15–21; Wisdom 9. 13–17
Acts 15. 23–29; Romans 8. 22–27; 1 Corinthians 12. 4–13
Psalms 25. 1–9; 104. 26–33; 143. 8–10
Luke 14. 27–33; John 14. 23–26; John 16. 13–15

The Commemoration of the Faithful Departed
Lamentations 3. 17–26, 31–3 *or* Wisdom 3. 1–9
Psalm 23 *or* Psalm 27. 1–6, 16–17
Romans 5. 5–11 *or* 1 Peter 1. 3–9
John 5. 19–25 *or* John 6. 37–40

Rogation Days
Deuteronomy 8. 1–10; 1 Kings 8. 35–40; Job 28. 1–11
Philippians 4. 4–7; 2 Thessalonians 3. 6–13; 1 John 5. 12–15
Psalms 104. 21–30; 107. 1–9; 121
Matthew 6. 1–15; Mark 11. 22–24; Luke 11. 5–13

Harvest Thanksgiving
Year A
Deuteronomy 8. 7–18 *or* Deuteronomy 28. 1–14
Psalm 65
2 Corinthians 9. 6–15
Luke 12. 16–30 *or* Luke 17. 11–19

Year B
Joel 2. 21–27
Psalm 126
1 Timothy 2. 1–7 *or* 1 Timothy 6. 6–10
Matthew 6. 25–33

Year C
Deuteronomy 26. 1–11
Psalm 100
Philippians 4. 4–9 *or* Revelation 14. 14–18
John 6. 25–35

Mission and Evangelism
Isaiah 49. 1–6; Isaiah 52. 7–10; Micah 4. 1–5
Acts 17. 12–34; 2 Corinthians 5.14 –6.2; Ephesians 2. 13–22
Psalms 2; 46; 67
Matthew 5. 13–16; Matthew 28. 16–20; John 17. 20–26

The Unity of the Church
Jeremiah 33. 6–9a; Ezekiel 36. 23–28; Zephaniah 3. 16–20
Ephesians 4. 1–6; Colossians 3. 9–17; 1 John 4. 9–15
Psalms 100; 122; 133
Matthew 18. 19–22; John 11. 45–52; John 17. 11b–23

The Peace of the World
Isaiah 9. 1–6; Isaiah 57. 15–19; Micah 4. 1–5
Philippians 4. 6–9; 1 Timothy 2. 1–6; James 3. 13–18
Psalms 40. 14–17; 72. 1–7; 85. 8–13
Matthew 5. 43–48; John 14. 23–29; John 15. 9–17

Social Justice and Responsibility
Isaiah 32. 15–20; Amos 5. 21–24; Amos 8. 4–7; Acts 5. 1–11
Colossians 3. 12–15; James 2. 1–4
Psalms 31. 21–24; 85. 1–7; 146. 5–10
Matthew 5. 1–12; Matthew 25. 31–46; Luke 16. 19–31

Ministry (including Ember Days)
Numbers 11. 16–17, 24–29; Numbers 27. 15–23; 1 Samuel 16. 1–13a
Isaiah 6. 1–8; Isaiah 61. 1–3; Jeremiah 1. 4–10
Acts 20. 28–35; 1 Corinthians 3. 3–11; Ephesians 4. 4–16; Philippians 3. 7–14
Psalms 40. 8–13; 84. 8–12; 89. 19–25; 101. 1–5, 7; 122
Luke 4. 16–21; Luke 12. 35–43; Luke 22. 24–27; John 4. 31–38; John 15. 5–17

In Time of Trouble
Genesis 9. 8–17; Job 1. 13–22; Isaiah 38. 6–11
Romans 3. 21–26; Romans 8. 18–25; 2 Corinthians 8. 1–5, 9
Psalms 86. 1–7; 107. 4–15; 142. 1–7
Mark 4. 35–41; Luke 12. 1–7; John 16. 31–33

For the Sovereign
Joshua 1. 1–9; Proverbs 8. 1–16
Romans 13. 1–10; Revelation 21.22 – 22.4
Psalms 20; 101; 121
Matthew 22. 16–22; Luke 22. 24–30

November 2005

| | Sunday Principal Service / Weekday Eucharist | Third Service / Morning Prayer |

27 **S** THE FIRST SUNDAY OF ADVENT
CW Year B begins

Isa. 64. 1–9	Ps. 44
Ps. 80. 1–8 [18–end]	Isa. 2. 1–5
1 Cor. 1. 3–9	Luke 12. 35–48
P | Mark 13. 24–end | |

28 **M** CW Weekday Lectionary Year 2 begins
Daily Eucharistic Lectionary Isa. 2. 1–5a   Ps. *50*; 54
Year 2 begins   Ps. 122   *alt.* Ps. *1*; 2; 3
Matt. 8. 5–11   Isa. 25. 1–9
P   Matt. 12. 1–21

29 **Tu**
Isa. 11. 1–10   Ps. *80*; 82
Ps. 72. 1–4, 18–19   *alt.* Ps. *5*; 6; (8)
Luke 10. 21–24   Isa. 26. 1–13
    Matt. 12. 22–37

Day of Intercession and Thanksgiving for the Missionary Work of the Church
Isa. 49. 1–6; Isa. 52. 7–10; Mic. 4. 1–5
Acts 17. 12–end; 2 Cor. 5.14 – 6.2; Eph. 2. 13–end
Ps. 2; 46; 47
Matt. 5. 13–16; Matt. 28. 16–end; John 17. 20–end
P

30 **W** ANDREW THE APOSTLE

Isa. 52. 7–10	*MP:* Ps. 47; 147. 1–12
Ps. 19. 1–6	Ezek. 47. 1–12
Rom. 10. 12–18	*or* Ecclus. 14. 20–end
R | Matt. 4. 18–22 | John 12. 20–32 |

December 2005

1 **Th** *Charles de Foucauld, Hermit in the Sahara, 1916*

Isa. 26. 1–6	Ps. *42*; 43
Ps. 118. 18–27a	*alt.* Ps. 14; *15*; 16
Matt. 7. 21, 24–27	Isa. 28. 14–end
P | | Matt. 13. 1–23 |

2 **F**

Isa. 29. 17–end	Ps. *25*; 26
Ps. 27. 1–4, 16–17	*alt.* Ps. 17; *19*
Matt. 9. 27–31	Isa. 29. 1–14
P | | Matt. 13. 24–43 |

3 **Sa** *Francis Xavier, Missionary, Apostle of the Indies, 1552*

Isa. 30. 19–21, 23–26	Ps. *9*; (10)
Ps. 146. 4–9	*alt.* Ps. 20; 21; *23*
Matt. 9.35 – 10.1, 6–8	Isa. 29. 15–end
P | | Matt. 13. 44–end |

4 **S** THE SECOND SUNDAY OF ADVENT

Isa. 40. 1–11	Ps. 80
Ps. 85. [1–2] 8–end	Baruch ch. 5
2 Pet. 3. 8–15a	*or* Zeph. 3. 14–end
P | Mark 1. 1–8 | Luke 1. 5–20 |

5 **M**

Isa. ch. 35	Ps. 44
Ps. 85. 7–end	*alt.* Ps. 27; *30*
Luke 5. 17–26	Isa. 30. 1–18
P | | Matt. 14. 1–12 |

6 **Tu** **Nicholas, Bishop of Myra, *c.* 326**
Com. Bishop   *or* Isa. 40. 1–11   Ps. *56*; 57
also Isa. 61. 1–3   Ps. 96. 1, 10–end   *alt.* Ps. 32; *36*
1 Tim. 6. 6–11   Matt. 18. 12–14   Isa. 30. 19–end
Pw Mark 10. 13–16   Matt. 14. 13–end

Second Service Evening Prayer		Calendar and Holy Communion	Morning Prayer	Evening Prayer
		THE FIRST SUNDAY IN ADVENT Advent 1 Coll. until Christmas Eve		
Ps. 25. 1–9 [10–end] Isa. 1. 1–20 Matt. 21. 1–13		Mic. 4. 1–4, 6–7 Ps. 25. 1–9 Rom. 13. 8–14 **P** Matt. 21. 1–13	Ps. 44 Isa. 2. 1–5 Luke 12. 35–48	Ps. 9 Isa. 1. 1–20 Mark 13. 24–end
Ps. 70; *71* *alt.* Ps. *4*; 7 Isa. 42. 18–end Rev. ch. 19		**P**	Isa. 25. 1–9 Matt. 12. 1–21	Isa. 42. 18–end Rev. ch. 19
Ps. *74*; 75 *alt.* *9*; 10† Isa. 43. 1–13 Rev. ch. 20 *or First EP of Andrew* Ps. 48 Isa. 49. 1–9a 1 Cor. 4. 9–16 **R** ct			Isa. 26. 1–13 Matt. 12. 22–37	Isa. 43. 1–13 Rev. ch. 20 *or First EP of Andrew* (Ps. 48) Isa. 49. 1–9a 1 Cor. 4. 9–16 **R** ct
		P To celebrate the Day of Intercession and Thanksgiving for the Missionary Work of the Church, see *Common Worship* provision.		
EP: Ps. 87; 96 Zech. 8. 20–end John 1. 35–42		**ANDREW THE APOSTLE** Zech. 8. 20–end Ps. 92. 1–5 Rom. 10. 9–end **R** Matt. 4. 18–22	(Ps. 47; 147. 1–12) Ezek. 47. 1–12 *or* Ecclus. 14. 20–end John 12. 20–32	(Ps. 87; 96) Isa. 52. 7–10 John 1. 35–42
Ps. *40*; 46 *alt.* Ps. 18† Isa. 44. 1–8 Rev. 21. 9–21		**P**	Isa. 28. 14–end Matt. 13. 1–23	Isa. 44. 1–8 Rev. 21. 9–21
Ps. 16; *17* *alt.* Ps. 22 Isa. 44. 9–23 Rev. 21.22 – 22.5		**P**	Isa. 29. 1–14 Matt. 13. 24–43	Isa. 44. 9–23 Rev. 21.22 – 22.5
Ps. *27*; 28 *alt.* Ps. *24*; 25 Isa. 44.24 – 45.13 Rev. 22. 6–end ct		**P**	Isa. 29. 15–end Matt. 13. 44–end	Isa. 44.24 – 45.13 Rev. 22. 6–end ct
Ps. 40. [1–10] 12–end 1 Kings 22. 1–28 Rom. 15. 4–13 *Gospel:* Matt. 11. 2–11		**THE SECOND SUNDAY IN ADVENT** 2 Kings 22. 8–10; 23. 1–3 Ps. 50. 1–6 Rom. 15. 4–13 **P** Luke 21. 25–33	Ps. 80 Baruch ch. 5 *or* Zeph. 3. 14–end Luke 1. 5–20	Ps. 40. [1–10] 12–end 1 Kings 22. 1–28 2 Pet. 3. 8–15a
Ps. *144*; 146 *alt.* Ps. 26; *28*; 29 Isa. 45. 14–end 1 Thess. ch. 1		**P**	Isa. 30. 1–18 Matt. 14. 1–12	Isa. 45. 14–end 1 Thess. ch. 1
Ps. *11*; 12; 13 *alt.* Ps. 33 Isa. ch. 46 1 Thess. 2. 1–12		**Nicholas, Bishop of Myra,** *c.* **326** Com. Bishop **Pw**	Isa. 30. 19–end Matt. 14. 13–end	Isa. ch. 46 1 Thess. 2. 1–12

December 2005

| | Sunday Principal Service / Weekday Eucharist | Third Service / Morning Prayer |

7 W   **Ambrose, Bishop of Milan, Teacher, 397**
Ember Day*
Com. Teacher	*or* Isa. 40. 25–end	Ps. *62*; 63
also Isa. 41. 9b–13	Ps. 103. 8–13	*alt.* Ps. 34
Luke 22. 24–30	Matt. 11. 28–end	Isa. ch. 31
Pw		Matt. 15. 1–20

8 Th   **The Conception of the Blessed Virgin Mary**
Com. BVM	*or* Isa. 41. 13–20	Ps. 53; *54*; 60
	Ps. 145. 1, 8–13	*alt.* Ps. 37†
	Matt. 11. 11–15	Isa. ch. 32
Pw		Matt. 15. 21–28

9 F   Ember Day*
	Isa. 48. 17–19	Ps. 85; *86*
	Ps. 1	*alt.* Ps. 31
	Matt. 11. 16–19	Isa. 33. 1–22
P		Matt. 15. 29–end

10 Sa   Ember Day*
	Ecclus. 48. 1–4, 9–11	Ps. 145
	or 2 Kings 2. 9–12	*alt.* Ps. 41; *42*; 43
	Ps. 80. 1–4, 18–19	Isa. ch. 35
	Matt. 17. 10–13	Matt. 16. 1–12
P		

11 S   THE THIRD SUNDAY OF ADVENT
	Isa. 61. 1–4, 8–11	Ps. 50. 1–6, 62
	Ps. 126	Isa. ch. 12
	or Canticle: Magnificat	Luke 1. 57–66
	1 Thess. 5. 16–24	
P	John 1. 6–8, 19–28	

12 M
	Num. 24. 2–7, 15–17	Ps. 40
	Ps. 25. 3–8	*alt.* Ps. 44
	Matt. 21. 23–27	Isa. 38. 1–8, 21–22
P		Matt. 16. 13–end

13 Tu   **Lucy, Martyr at Syracuse, 304**
Samuel Johnson, Moralist, 1784
Com. Martyr	*or* Zeph. 3. 1–2, 9–13	Ps. *70*; 74
also Wisd. 3. 1–7	Ps. 34. 1–6, 21–22	*alt.* Ps. *48*; 52
2 Cor. 4. 6–15	Matt. 21. 28–32	Isa. 38. 9–20
Pr		Matt. 17. 1–13

14 W   **John of the Cross, Poet, Teacher, 1591**
Com. Teacher	*or* Isa. 45. 6b–8, 18, 21b–end	Ps. *75*; 96
esp. 1 Cor. 2. 1–10	Ps. 85. 7–end	*alt.* Ps. 119. 57–80
also John 14. 18–23	Luke 7. 18b–23	Isa. ch. 39
Pw		Matt. 17. 14–21

15 Th
	Isa. 54. 1–10	Ps. *76*; 97
	Ps. 30. 1–5, 11–end	*alt.* Ps. 56; *57*; (63†)
	Luke 7. 24–30	Zeph. 1.1 – 2.3
P		Matt. 17. 22–end

16 F
	Isa. 56. 1–3a, 6–8	Ps. 77; *98*
	Ps. 67	*alt.* Ps. *51*; 54
	John 5. 33–36	Zeph. 3. 1–13
P		Matt. 18. 1–20

17 Sa   O Sapientia
Eglantine Jebb, Social Reformer, Founder of 'Save the Children', 1928
	Gen. 49. 2, 8–10	Ps. 71
	Ps. 72. 1–5, 18–19	*alt.* Ps. 68
	Matt. 1. 1–17	Zeph. 3. 14–end
P		Matt. 18. 21–end

*For Ember Day provision, see p. 13.

Second Service Evening Prayer	Calendar and Holy Communion	Morning Prayer	Evening Prayer
Ps. *10*; 14 *alt.* Ps. 119. 33–56 Isa. ch. 47 1 Thess. 2. 13–end P		Isa. ch. 31 Matt. 15. 1–20	Isa. ch. 47 1 Thess. 2. 13–end
Ps. 73 *alt.* Ps. 39; *40* Isa. 48. 1–11 1 Thess. ch. 3 Pw	The Conception of the Blessed Virgin Mary Isa. ch. 32 Matt. 15. 21–28	Isa. 48. 1–11	Isa. 48. 1–11 1 Thess. ch. 3
Ps. 82; *90* *alt.* Ps. 35 Isa. 48. 12–end 1 Thess. 4. 1–12 P		Isa. 33. 1–22 Matt. 15. 29–end	Isa. 48. 12–end 1 Thess. 4. 1–12
Ps. 93; *94* *alt.* Ps. 45; *46* Isa. 49. 1–13 1 Thess. 4. 13–end ct P		Isa. ch. 35 Matt. 16. 1–12	Isa. 49. 1–13 1 Thess. 4. 13–end ct
Ps. 68. 1–8 [9–19] Mal. 3. 1–4; ch. 4 Phil. 4. 4–7 *Gospel:* Matt. 14. 1–12 P	THE THIRD SUNDAY IN ADVENT Isa. 35. 1–10 Ps. 80. 1–7 1 Cor. 4. 1–5 Matt. 11. 2–10	Ps. 62 Isa. ch. 12 Luke 1. 57–66	Ps. 68. 1–8 [9–20] Mal. 3. 1–4; ch. 4 Matt. 14. 1–12
Ps. 25; *26* *alt.* Ps. *47*; 49 Isa. 49. 14–25 1 Thess. 5. 1–11 P		Isa. 38. 1–8, 21–22 Matt. 16. 13–end	Isa. 49. 14–25 1 Thess. 5. 1–11
Ps. *50*; 54 *alt.* Ps. 50 Isa. ch. 50 1 Thess. 5. 12–end Pr	Lucy, Martyr at Syracuse, 304 Com. Virgin Martyr	Isa. 38. 9–20 Matt. 17. 1–13	Isa. ch. 50 1 Thess. 5. 12–end
Ps. 25; *82* *alt.* Ps. *59*; 60; (67) Isa. 51. 1–8 2 Thess. ch. 1 P	Ember Day Ember CEG	Isa. ch. 39 Matt. 17. 14–21	Isa. 51. 1–8 2 Thess. ch. 1
Ps. 44 *alt.* Ps. 61; *62*; 64 Isa. 51. 9–16 2 Thess. ch. 2 P		Zeph. 1.1 – 2.3 Matt. 17. 22–end	Isa. 51. 9–16 2 Thess. ch. 2
Ps. 49 *alt.* Ps. 38 Isa. 51. 17–end 2 Thess. ch. 3 P	Ember Day O Sapientia Ember CEG	Zeph. 3. 1–13 Matt. 18. 1–20	Isa. 51. 17–end 2 Thess. ch. 3
Ps. 42; *43* *alt.* Ps. 65; *66* Isa. 52. 1–12 Jude ct P	Ember Day Ember CEG	Zeph. 3. 14–end Matt. 18. 21–end	Isa. 52. 1–12 Jude ct

December 2005

	Sunday Principal Service Weekday Eucharist	Third Service Morning Prayer

18 S   THE FOURTH SUNDAY OF ADVENT

	2 Sam. 7. 1–11, 16	Ps. 144
	Canticle: Magnificat	Isa. 7. 10–16
	or Ps. 89. 1–4, 19–26 (*or* 1–8)	Rom. 1. 1–7
	Rom. 16. 25–end	
P	Luke 1. 26–38	

19 M

	Judg. 13. 2–7, 24–end	Ps. 144; *146*
	Ps. 71. 3–8	Mal. 1. 1, 6–end
P	Luke 1. 5–25	Matt. 19. 1–12

20 Tu

	Isa. 7. 10–14	Ps. *46*; 95
	Ps. 24. 1–6	Mal. 2. 1–16
	Luke 1. 26–38	Matt. 19. 13–15

P

21 W*

	Zeph. 3. 14–18	Ps. *121*; 122; 123
	Ps. 33. 1–4, 11–12, 19–end	Mal. 2.17 – 3.12
P	Luke 1. 39–45	Matt. 19. 16–end

22 Th

	1 Sam. 1. 24–end	Ps. *124*; 125; 126; 127
	Ps. 113	Mal. 3.13 – 4.end
P	Luke 1. 46–56	Matt. 23. 1–12

23 F

	Mal. 3. 1–4; 4. 5–end	Ps. 128; 129; *130*; 131
	Ps. 25. 3–9	Nahum ch. 1
P	Luke 1. 57–66	Matt. 23. 13–28

24 Sa   CHRISTMAS EVE

	Morning Eucharist	Ps. *45*; 113
	2 Sam. 7. 1–5, 8–11, 16	Obadiah
	Ps. 89. 2, 19–27	Matt. 23. 29–end
	Acts 13. 16–26	
	Luke 1. 67–79	

P

25 S   CHRISTMAS DAY

Any of the following sets of	I	Ps. *110*; 117
readings may be used on the	Isa. 9. 2–7	Isa. 62. 1–5
evening of Christmas Eve	Ps. 96	Matt. 1. 18–end
and on Christmas Day.	Titus 2. 11–14	
Set III should be used at	Luke 2. 1–14 [15–20]	
some service during the	II	
celebration.	Isa. 62. 6–end	
	Ps. 97	
	Titus 3. 4–7	
	Luke 2. [1–7] 8–20	
	III	
	Isa. 52. 7–10	
	Ps. 98	
	Heb. 1. 1–4 [5–12]	
ꟿ	John 1. 1–14	

26 M   STEPHEN, DEACON, FIRST MARTYR

The reading from Acts must	2 Chron. 24. 20–22	*MP*: Ps. *13*; 31. 1–8; 150
be used as either the first or	*or* Acts 7. 51–end	Jer. 26. 12–15
second reading at the	Ps. 119. 161–168	Acts ch. 6
Eucharist.	Acts 7. 51–60	
	or Gal. 2. 16b–20	
	Matt. 10. 17–22	

R

*Thomas the Apostle may be celebrated on 21 December instead of 3 July.

Second Service Evening Prayer	Calendar and Holy Communion	Morning Prayer	Evening Prayer
Ps. 113 [131] Zech. 2. 10–end Luke 1. 39–55	**THE FOURTH SUNDAY IN ADVENT** Isa. 40. 1–9 Ps. 145. 17–end Phil. 4. 4–7 John 1. 19–28 **P**	Ps. 144 Isa. 7. 10–16 Rom. 1. 1–7	Ps. 113; [131] Zech. 2. 10–end Luke 1. 39–55
Ps. 10; *57* Isa. 52.13 – 53.end 2 Pet. 1. 1–15	**P**	Mal. 1. 1, 6–end Matt. 19. 1–12	Isa. 52.13 – 53.end 2 Pet. 1–15
Ps. *4*; 9 Isa. ch. 54 2 Pet. 1.16 – 2.3	**P**	Mal. 2. 1–16 Matt. 19. 13–15	Isa. ch. 54 2 Pet. 1.16 – 2.3 *or First EP of Thomas* (Ps. 27) Isa. ch. 35 Heb. 10.35 – 11.1 **R ct**
Ps. 80; *84* Isa. ch. 55 2 Pet. 2. 4–end	**THOMAS THE APOSTLE** Job 42. 1–6 Ps. 139. 1–11 Eph. 2. 19–end **R** John 20. 24–end	(Ps. 92; 146) 2 Sam. 15. 17–21 *or* Ecclus. ch. 2 John 11. 1–16	(Ps. 139) Hab. 2. 1–4 1 Pet. 1. 3–12
Ps. 24; *48* Isa. 56. 1–8 2 Pet. ch. 3	**P**	Mal. 3.13 – 4.end Matt. 23. 1–12	Isa. 56. 1–8 2 Pet. ch. 3
Ps. 89. 1–37 Isa. 63. 1–6 2 John	**P**	Nahum ch. 1 Matt. 23. 13–28	Isa. 63. 1–6 2 John
Ps. 85 Zech. ch. 2 Rev. 1. 1–8	**CHRISTMAS EVE** Coll. (1) Christmas Eve (2) Advent 1 Mic. 5. 2–5a Ps. 24 Titus 3. 3–7 **P** Luke 2. 1–14	Ps. 45; 113 Obadiah Matt. 23. 29–end	Ps. 85 Zech. ch. 2 Rev. 1. 1–8
Ps. 8 Isa. 65. 17–25 Phil. 2. 5–11 *or* Luke 2. 1–20 *if it has not been used at the Principal Service of the day*	**CHRISTMAS DAY** Isa. 9. 2–7 Ps. 98 Heb. 1. 1–12 John 1. 1–14 ₩	Ps. *110*; 117 Isa. 62. 1–5 Matt. 1. 18–end	Ps. 8 Isa. 65. 17–25 Phil. 2. 5–11 *or* Luke 2. 1–20
EP: Ps. 57; *86* Gen. 4. 1–10 Matt. 23. 34–end	**STEPHEN, DEACON, FIRST MARTYR** Coll. (1) Stephen (2) Christmas 2 Chron. 24. 20–22 Ps. 119. 161–168 Acts 7. 55–end **R** Matt. 23. 34–end	(Ps. 13; 31. 1–8; 150) Jer. 26. 12–15 Acts ch. 6	(Ps. 57; 86) Gen. 4. 1–10 Matt. 10. 17–22

December 2005	Sunday Principal Service Weekday Eucharist	Third Service Morning Prayer

27	Tu	JOHN, APOSTLE AND EVANGELIST Exod. 33. 7–11a Ps. 117 1 John ch. 1 John 21. 19b–end	*MP:* Ps. *21*; 147. 13–end Exod. 33. 12–end 1 John 2. 1–11
	W		
28	W W	THE HOLY INNOCENTS Jer. 31. 15–17 Ps. 124 1 Cor. 1. 26–29 Matt. 2. 13–18	*MP:* Ps. *36*; 146 Baruch 4. 21–27 *or* Gen. 37. 13–20 Matt. 18. 1–10
	R		
29	Th Wr	Thomas Becket, Archbishop of Canterbury, Martyr, 1170* Com. Martyr *or* 1 John 2. 3–11 *esp*. Matt. 10. 28–33 Ps. 96. 1–4 *also* Ecclus. 51. 1–8 Luke 2. 22–35	Ps. *19*; 20 Jonah ch. 1 Col. 1. 1–14
30	F W	1 John 2. 12–17 Ps. 96. 7–10 Luke 2. 36–40	Ps. 111; 112; *113* Jonah ch. 2 Col. 1. 15–23
31	Sa	*John Wyclif, Reformer, 1384* 1 John 2. 18–21 Ps. 96. 1, 11–end John 1. 1–18	Ps. 102 Jonah chs. 3 and 4 Col. 1.24 – 2.7
	W		

January 2006

1	S W	THE NAMING AND CIRCUMCISION OF JESUS (*or* transferred to 2nd) Num. 6. 22–end Ps. 8 Gal. 4. 4–7 Luke 2. 15–21	*MP:* Ps. *103*; 150 Gen. 17. 1–13 Rom. 2. 17–end
		or, for The Second Sunday of Christmas: Isa. 61.10 – 62.3 Ps. 148. [1–6] 7–end Gal. 4. 4–7	Ps. 105. 1–11 Isa. 63. 7–9 Eph. 3. 5–12
	W	Luke 2. 15–21	
2	M W	For The Naming and Circumcision of Jesus, see 1st **Basil the Great and Gregory of Nazianzus, Bishops, Teachers, 379 and 389** *Seraphim, Monk of Sarov, Spiritual Guide, 1833; Vedanayagam Samuel Azariah, Bishop in South India, Evangelist, 1945* Com. Teacher *or* 1 John 2. 22–28 *esp*. 2 Tim. 4. 1–8 Ps. 98. 1–4 Matt. 5. 13–19 John 1. 19–28	Ps. 18. 1–30 Ruth ch. 1 Col. 2. 8–end
3	Tu W	1 John 2.29 – 3.6 Ps. 98. 2–7 John 1. 29–34	Ps. *127*; 128; 131 Ruth ch. 2 Col. 3. 1–11
4	W W	1 John 3. 7–10 Ps. 98. 1, 8–end John 1. 35–42	Ps. 89. 1–37 Ruth ch. 3 Col 3.12 – 4.1

* Thomas Becket may be celebrated on 7 July instead of 29 December.

Second Service Evening Prayer		Calendar and Holy Communion	Morning Prayer	Evening Prayer
EP: Ps. 97 Isa. 6. 1–8 1 John 5. 1–12	 W	**JOHN, APOSTLE AND EVANGELIST** Coll. (1) John (2) Christmas Exod. 33. 18–end Ps. 92. 11–end 1 John ch. 1 John 21. 19b–end	(Ps. 21; 147. 13–end) Exod. 33. 7–11a 1 John 2. 1–11	(Ps. 97) Isa. 6. 1–8 1 John 5. 1–12
EP: Ps. 123; *128* Isa. 49. 14–25 Mark 10. 13–16	 R	**THE HOLY INNOCENTS** Coll. (1) Innocents (2) Christmas Jer. 31. 10–17 Ps. 123 Rev. 14. 1–5 Matt. 2. 13–18	(Ps. 36; 146) Baruch 4. 21–27 *or* Gen. 37. 13–20 Matt. 18. 1–10	(Ps. 124; *128*) Isa. 49. 14–25 Mark 10. 13–16
Ps. 131; *132* Isa. 57. 15–end John 1. 1–18	 W	CEG of Christmas	Jonah ch. 1 Col. 1. 1–14	Isa. 57. 15–end John 1. 1–18
Ps. *65*; 84 Isa. 59. 1–15a John 1. 19–28	 W	CEG of Christmas	Jonah ch. 2 Col. 1. 15–23	Isa. 59. 1–15a John 1. 19–28
Ps. *90*; 148 Isa. 59. 15b–end John 1. 29–34 ct *or First EP of The Naming of Jesus* Ps. 148 Jer. 23. 1–6 Col. 2. 8–15 ct	 W	**Silvester, Bishop of Rome, 335** Com. Bishop	Jonah chs. 3 and 4 Col. 1.24 – 2.7	Isa. 59. 15b–end John 1. 29–34 ct *or First EP of The Circumcision of Christ* (Ps. 148) Jer. 23. 1–6 Col. 2. 8–15 ct
EP: Ps. 115 Deut. 30. [1–10] 11–20 Acts 3. 1–16	 W	**THE CIRCUMCISION OF CHRIST (*or* transferred to 2nd)** Additional collect Gen. 17. 3b–10 Ps. 98 Rom. 4. 8–14 *or* Eph. 2. 11–18 Luke 2. 15–21	Ps. 103; 150 Gen. 17. 1–13 Rom. 2. 17–end	Ps. 115 Deut. 30. [1–10] 11–20 Acts 3. 1–16
Ps. 132 Isa. ch. 35 Col. 1. 9–20 *or* Luke 2. 41–52	 W	*or, for The First Sunday after Christmas:* Isa. 62. 10–12 Ps. 45. 1–7 Gal. 4. 1–7 Matt. 1. 18–end	Ps. 105. 1–11 Isa. 63. 7–9 Eph. 3. 5–12	Ps. 132 Isa. ch. 35 1 John 1. 1–7
Ps. 45; *46* Isa. 60. 1–12 John 1. 35–42	 W		Ruth ch. 1 Col. 2. 8–end	Isa. 60. 1–12 John 1. 35–42
Ps. *2*; 110 Isa. 60. 13–end John 1. 43–end	 W		Ruth ch. 2 Col. 3. 1–11	Isa. 60. 13–end John 1. 43–end
Ps. 85; *87* Isa. ch. 61 John 2. 1–12	 W		Ruth ch. 3 Col 3.12 – 4.1	Isa. ch. 61 John 2. 1–12

January 2006

		Sunday Principal Service Weekday Eucharist	Third Service Morning Prayer

5 Th

1 John 3. 11–21
Ps. 100
John 1. 43–end

Ps. 8; *48*
Ruth 4. 1–17
Col. 4. 2–end

W

6 F   **THE EPIPHANY**

Isa. 60. 1–6
Ps. 72. [1–9] 10–15
Eph. 3. 1–12
꽝   Matt. 2. 1–12

MP: Ps. *132*; 113
Jer. 31. 7–14
John 1. 29–34

or, if The Epiphany is celebrated on 8 January:
1 John 5. 5–13
Ps. 147. 13–end
Mark 1. 7–11

Ps. *46*; 147. 13–end
Baruch 1.15 – 2.10
or Jer. 23. 1–8
W   Matt. 20. 1–16

7 Sa

1 John 3.22 – 4.6
Ps. 2. 7–end
Matt. 4. 12–17, 23–end

Ps. *99*; 147. 1–12
alt. Ps. *76*; 79*
Baruch 1.15 – 2.10
or Jer. 23. 1–8
Matt. 20. 1–16

W

or, if The Epiphany is celebrated on 8 January:
1 John 5. 14–21
Ps. 149. 1–5
John 2. 1–11

Ps. *99*; 147. 1–12
Baruch 2. 11–end
or Jer. 30. 1–17
W   Matt. 20. 17–28

8 S   **THE BAPTISM OF CHRIST (The First Sunday of Epiphany)**
(or transferred to 9 January if The Epiphany is celebrated today. For The Epiphany, see provision on the 6th)

Gen. 1. 1–5
Ps. 29
Acts 19. 1–7
꽝   Mark 1. 4–11

Ps. 89. 19–29
1 Sam. 16. 1–3, 13
John 1. 29–34

9 M   For The Baptism, see provision on the 8th.
DEL 1   1 Sam. 1. 1–8
Ps. 116. 10–15
W   Mark 1. 14–20

Ps. *2*; 110
alt. Ps. *80*; 82
Gen. 1. 1–19
Matt. 21. 1–17

10 Tu   *William Laud, Archbishop of Canterbury, 1645*
1 Sam. 1. 9–20
Canticle: 1 Sam. 2. 1, 4–8
or Magnificat
W   Mark 1. 21–28

Ps. 8; *9*
alt. Ps. 87; *89. 1–18*
Gen. 1.20 – 2.3
Matt. 21. 18–32

11 W   *Mary Slessor, Missionary in West Africa, 1915*
1 Sam. 3. 1–10, 19–20
Ps. 40. 1–4, 7–10
W   Mark 1. 29–39

Ps. 19; *20*
alt. Ps. 119. 105–128
Gen. 2. 4–end
Matt. 21. 33–end

12 Th   **Aelred of Hexham, Abbot of Rievaulx, 1167**
Benedict Biscop, Abbot of Wearmouth, Scholar, 689
Com. Religious   *or* 1 Sam. 4. 1–11
also Ecclus. 15. 1–6   Ps. 44. 10–15, 24–25
W   Mark 1. 40–end

Ps. *21*; 24
alt. Ps. 90; *92*
Gen. ch. 3
Matt. 22. 1–14

---

*Alt. psalm cycle begins on 9th if The Epiphany is celebrated on 8th.

Second Service Evening Prayer	Calendar and Holy Communion	Morning Prayer	Evening Prayer
First EP of The Epiphany Ps. 96; *97* Isa. 49. 1–13 John 4. 7–26 ☿ ct *or, if The Epiphany is celebrated on 8 January:* Ps. 96; *97* Isa. ch. 62 John 2. 13–end	W	Ruth 4. 1–17 Col. 4. 2–end	*First EP of The Epiphany* Ps. 96; *97* Isa. 49. 1–13 John 4. 7–26 ☿ ct
EP: Ps. *98*; 100 Baruch 4.36 – 5.end *or* Isa. 60. 1–9 John 2. 1–11	**THE EPIPHANY** Isa. 60. 1–9 Ps. 100 Eph. 3. 1–12 Matt. 2. 1–12	Ps. 132; 113 Jer. 31. 7–14 John 1. 29–34	Ps. 72; 98 Baruch 4.36 – 5.end *or* Isa. 60. 1–9 John 2. 1–11
Ps. 145 Isa. 63. 7–end 1 John ch. 3	☿		
Ps. 118 *alt.* Ps. 81; *84* Isa. 63. 7–end 1 John ch. 3 ct *or First EP of The Baptism of Christ* Ps. 36 Isa. ch. 61 Titus 2. 11–14; 3. 4–7 ☿ ct *First EP of The Epiphany* Ps. 96; *97* Isa. 49. 1–13 John 4. 7–26 ☿ ct	W *or* G	Baruch 1.15 – 2.10 *or* Jer. 23. 1–8 Matt. 20. 1–16	Isa. 63. 7–end 1 John ch. 3 ct
Ps. 46 [47] Isa. 42 1–9 Eph. 2. 1–10 *Gospel:* Matt. 3. 13–17	**THE FIRST SUNDAY AFTER EPIPHANY** To celebrate The Baptism of Christ, see *Common Worship* provision. Zech. 8. 1–8 Ps. 72. 1–8 Rom. 12. 1–5 Luke 2. 41–end W *or* G	Ps. 89. 19–29 1 Sam. 16. 1–3, 13 John 1. 29–34	Ps. 46 [47] Isa. 42 1–9 Eph. 2. 1–10
Ps. *34*; 36 *alt.* Ps. *85*; 86 Amos ch. 1 1 Cor. 1. 1–17	W *or* G	Gen. 1. 1–19 Matt. 21. 1–17	Amos ch. 1 1 Cor. 1. 1–17
Ps. *45*; 46 *alt.* Ps. 89. 19–end Amos ch. 2 1 Cor. 1. 18–end	W *or* G	Gen. 1.20 – 2.3 Matt. 21. 18–32	Amos. ch. 2 1 Cor. 1. 18–end
Ps. *47*; 48 *alt.* Ps. *91*; 93 Amos ch. 3 1 Cor. ch. 2	W *or* G	Gen. 2. 4–end Matt. 21. 33–end	Amos ch. 3 1 Cor. ch. 2
Ps. *61*; 65 *alt.* Ps. 94 Amos ch. 4 1 Cor. ch. 3	W *or* G	Gen. ch. 3 Matt. 22. 1–14	Amos ch. 4 1 Cor. ch. 3

January 2006

	Sunday Principal Service / Weekday Eucharist	Third Service / Morning Prayer

13 F **Hilary, Bishop of Poitiers, Teacher, 367**
Kentigern (Mungo), Missionary Bishop in Strathclyde and Cumbria, 603; George Fox, Founder of the Society of Friends (the Quakers), 1691

Com. Teacher *or*	1 Sam. 8. 4–7, 10–end	Ps. *67*; 72
also 1 John 2. 18–25	Ps. 89. 15–18	*alt.* Ps. *88* (95)
John 8. 25–32	Mark 2. 1–12	Gen. 4. 1–16, 25–26
W		Matt. 22. 15–33

14 Sa

	1 Sam. 9. 1–4, 17–19; 10. 1	Ps. 29; *33*
	Ps. 21. 1–6	*alt.* Ps. 96; *97*; 100
	Mark 2. 13–17	Gen. 6. 1–10
W		Matt. 22. 34–end

15 S **THE SECOND SUNDAY OF EPIPHANY**

	1 Sam. 3. 1–10[11–20]	Ps. 145. 1–12
	Ps. 139. 1–5, 12–18 (*or* 1–9)	Isa. 62. 1–5
	Rev. 5. 1–10	1 Cor. 6. 11–end
W	John 1. 43–end	

16 M

	1 Sam. 15. 16–23	Ps. 145; *146*
DEL 2	Ps. 50. 8–10, 16–17, 24	*alt.* Ps. *98*; 99; 101
	Mark 2. 18–22	Gen. 6.11 – 7.10
W		Matt. 24. 1–14

17 Tu **Antony of Egypt, Hermit, Abbot, 356**
Charles Gore, Bishop, Founder of the Community of the Resurrection, 1932

Com. Religious *or*	1 Sam. 16. 1–13	Ps. *132*; 147. 1–12
esp. Phil. 3. 7–14	Ps. 89. 19–27	*alt.* Ps. 106† (*or* Ps. 103)
also Matt. 19. 16–26	Mark 2. 23–end	Gen. 7. 11–end
W		Matt. 24. 15–28

18 W The Week of Prayer for Christian Unity until 25th

	1 Sam. 17. 32–33, 37, 40–51	Ps. *81*; 147. 13–end
	Ps. 144. 1–2, 9–10	*alt.* Ps. 110; *111*; 112
	Mark 3. 1–6	Gen. 8. 1–14
W		Matt. 24. 29–end

19 Th **Wulfstan, Bishop of Worcester, 1095**

Com. Bishop *or*	1 Sam. 18. 6–9; 19. 1–7	Ps. 76; 148
esp. Matt. 24. 42–46	Ps. 56. 1–2, 8–end	*alt.* Ps. 113; *115*
	Mark 3. 7–12	Gen. 8.15 – 9.7
W		Matt. 25. 1–13

20 F *Richard Rolle of Hampole, Spiritual Writer, 1349*

	1 Sam. 24. 3–22a	Ps. *27*; Ps. 149
	Ps. 57. 1–2, 8–end	*alt.* Ps. 139
	Mark 3. 13–19	Gen. 9. 8–19
W		Matt. 25. 14–30

21 Sa **Agnes, Child Martyr at Rome, 304**

Com. Martyr *or*	2 Sam. 1. 1–4, 11–12, 17–19,	Ps. *122*; 128; 150
also Rev. 7. 13–17	23–end	*alt.* Ps. 120; *121*; 122
	Ps. 80. 1–6	Gen. 11. 1–9
	Mark 3. 20–21	Matt. 25. 31–end
Wr		

22 S **THE THIRD SUNDAY OF EPIPHANY**

	Gen. 14. 17–20	Ps. 113
	Ps. 128	Jonah 3. 1–5, 10
	Rev. 19. 6–10	John 3. 16–21
W	John 2. 1–11	

23 M

	2 Sam. 5. 1–7, 10	Ps. 40; *108*
DEL 3	Ps. 89. 19–27	*alt.* Ps. 123; 124; 125; *126*
	Mark 3. 22–30	Gen. 11.27 – 12.9
W		Matt. 26. 1–16

Second Service Evening Prayer	Calendar and Holy Communion	Morning Prayer	Evening Prayer
	Hilary, Bishop of Poitiers, Teacher, 367		
Ps. 68 *alt.* Ps. 102 Amos 5. 1–17 1 Cor. ch. 4	Com. Doctor W *or* Gw	Gen. 4. 1–16, 25–26 Matt. 22. 15–33	Amos 5. 1–17 1 Cor. ch. 4
Ps. 84; *85* *alt.* Ps. 104 Amos 5. 18–end 1 Cor. ch. 5 ct	 W *or* G	Gen. 6. 1–10 Matt. 22. 34–end	Amos 5. 18–end 1 Cor. ch. 5 ct
Ps. 96 Isa. 60. 9–end Heb. 6.17 – 7.10 *Gospel:* Matt. 8. 5–13	THE SECOND SUNDAY AFTER EPIPHANY 2 Kings 4. 1–17 Ps. 107. 13–22 Rom. 12. 6–16a John 2. 1–11 W *or* G	Ps. 145. 1–12 Isa. 62. 1–5 1 Cor. 6. 11–end	Ps. 96 Isa. 60. 9–end Heb. 6.17 – 7.10
Ps. 71 *alt.* Ps. 105† (*or* Ps. 103) Amos ch. 6 1 Cor. 6. 1–11	 W *or* G	Gen. 6.11 – 7.10 Matt. 24. 1–14	Amos ch. 6 1 Cor. 6. 1–11
Ps. 89. 1–37 *alt.* Ps. 107† Amos ch. 7 1 Cor. 6. 12–end	 W *or* G	Gen. 7. 11–end Matt. 24. 15–28	Amos ch. 7 1 Cor. 6. 12–end
Ps. *97*; 98 *alt.* Ps. 119. 129–152 Amos ch. 8 1 Cor. 7. 1–24	Prisca, Martyr at Rome, *c.* 265 For the Week of Prayer for Christian Unity, see *Common Worship* provision. Com. Virgin Martyr Wr *or* Gr	Gen. 8. 1–14 Matt. 24. 29–end	Amos ch. 8 1 Cor. 7. 1–24
Ps. 99; 100; *111* *alt.* Ps. 114; *116*; 117 Amos ch. 9 1 Cor. 7. 25–end	 W *or* G	Gen. 8.15 – 9.7 Matt. 25. 1–13	Amos ch. 9 1 Cor. 7. 25–end
Ps. 73 *alt.* Ps. *130*; 131; 137 Hos. 1.1 – 2.1 1 Cor. ch. 8	Fabian, Bishop of Rome, Martyr, 250 Com. Martyr Wr *or* Gr	Gen. 9. 8–19 Matt. 25. 14–30	Hos. 1.1 – 2.1 1 Cor. ch. 8
Ps. *61*; 66 *alt.* Ps. 118 Hos. 2. 2–17 1 Cor. 9. 1–14 ct	Agnes, Child Martyr at Rome, 304 Com. Virgin Martyr Wr *or* Gr	Gen. 11. 1–9 Matt. 25. 31–end	Hos. 2. 2–17 1 Cor. 9. 1–14 ct
Ps. 33. 1–12 [13–end] Jer. 3.21 – 4.2 Titus 2. 1–8, 11–14 *Gospel:* Matt. 4. 12–23	THE THIRD SUNDAY AFTER EPIPHANY 2 Kings 6. 14b–23 Ps. 102. 15–22 Rom. 12. 16b–end Matt. 8. 1–13 W *or* G	Ps. 113 Jonah 3. 1–5, 10 John 3. 16–21	Ps. 33. 1–12 [13–end] Jer. 3.21 – 4.2 Titus 2. 1–8, 11–14
Ps. *138*; 144 *alt.* Ps. *127*; 128; 129 Hos. 2.18 – 3.end 1 Cor. 9. 15–end	 W *or* G	Gen. 11.27 – 12.9 Matt. 26. 1–16	Hos. 2.18 – 3.end 1 Cor. 9. 15–end

January 2006

	Sunday Principal Service Weekday Eucharist	Third Service Morning Prayer

24 Tu **Francis de Sales, Bishop of Geneva, Teacher, 1274**
Com. Teacher *or* 2 Sam. 6. 12–15, 17–19   Ps. 34; *36*
also Prov. 3. 13–18   Ps. 24. 7–end   *alt.* Ps. *132*; 133
John 3. 17–21   Mark 3. 31–end   Gen. 13. 2–end
     Matt. 26. 17–35

W

25 W **THE CONVERSION OF PAUL**
The reading from Acts must   Jer. 1. 4–10   *MP:* Ps. 66; 147. 13–end
be used as either the first or   *or* Acts 9. 1–22   Ezek. 3. 22–end
second reading at the   Ps. 67   Phil. 3. 1–14
Eucharist.   Acts 9. 1–22
W   *or* Gal. 1. 11–16a
     Matt. 19. 27–end

26 Th **Timothy and Titus, Companions of Paul**
Isa. 61. 1–3a *or* 2 Sam. 7. 18–19, 24–end   Ps. *47*; 48
Ps. 100   Ps. 132. 1–5, 11–15   *alt.* Ps. *143*; 146
2 Tim. 2. 1–8   Mark 4. 21–25   Gen. ch. 15
or Titus 1. 1–5   Matt. 26. 47–56
W Luke 10. 1–9

27 F   2 Sam. 11. 1–10, 13–17   Ps. 61; *65*
     Ps. 51. 1–6, 9   *alt.* Ps. 142; *144*
W   Mark 4. 26–34   Gen. ch. 16
     Matt. 26. 57–end

28 Sa **Thomas Aquinas, Priest, Philosopher, Teacher, 1274**
Com. Teacher *or* 2 Sam. 12. 1–7, 10–17   Ps. 68
esp. Wisd. 7. 7–10, 15–16   Ps. 51. 11–16   *alt.* Ps. 147
1 Cor. 2. 9–end   Mark 4. 35–end   Gen. 17. 1–22
John 16. 12–15   Matt. 27. 1–10
W

29 S **THE FOURTH SUNDAY OF EPIPHANY**
or The Presentation of Christ in the Temple*
     Deut. 18. 15–20   Ps. 71. 1–6, 15–17
     Ps. 111   Jer. 1. 4–10
     Rev. 12. 1–5a   Mark 1. 40–end
     Mark 1. 21–28
W

30 M **Charles, King and Martyr, 1649**
Com. Martyr *or* 2 Sam. 15. 13–14, 30; 16. 5–13   Ps. *57*; 96***
DEL 4 *also* Ecclus. 2. 12–17   Ps. 3   *alt.* Ps. *1*; 2; 3
1 Tim. 6. 12–16   Mark 5. 1–20   Gen. 18. 1–15
Wr [Gr]**   Matt. 27. 11–26

31 Tu *John Bosco, Priest, Founder of the Salesian Teaching Order, 1888*
     2 Sam. 18. 9–10, 14, 24–25,   Ps. *93*; 97***
     30 – 19.3   *alt.* Ps. *5*; 6; (8)
     Ps. 86. 1–6   Gen. 18. 16–end
W [G]   Mark 5. 21–end   Matt. 27. 27–44

February 2006

1 W *Brigid, Abbess of Kildare, c. 525*
     2 Sam. 24. 2, 9–17   Ps. *95*; 98***
     Ps. 32. 1–8   *alt.* Ps. 119. 1–32
     Mark 6. 1–6a   Gen. 19. 1–3, 12–29
     Matt. 27. 45–56
W [G]

*See provision for First EP on 1 February and throughout the day for The Presentation on 2 February.
**Ordinary Time begins today if The Presentation was observed on 29th.
***If The Presentation was observed on 29th, the alternative psalms are used.

Second Service Evening Prayer	Calendar and Holy Communion	Morning Prayer	Evening Prayer
Ps. 145 *alt.* Ps. (134) *135* Hos. 4. 1–16 1 Cor. 10. 1–13 *or First EP of The Conversion of Paul* Ps. 149 Isa. 49. 1–13 Acts 22. 3–16 ct	W *or* G	Gen. 13. 2–end Matt. 26. 17–35	Hos. 4. 1–16 1 Cor. 10. 1–13 *or First EP of The Conversion of Paul* (Ps. 149) Isa. 49. 1–13 Acts 22. 3–16 W ct
	THE CONVERSION OF PAUL		
EP: Ps. 119. 41–56 Ecclus. 39. 1–10 *or* Isa. 56. 1–8 Col. 1.24 – 2.7	Josh. 5. 13–end Ps. 67 Acts 9. 1–22 Matt. 19. 27–end W	(Ps. 66; 147. 13–end) Ezek. 3. 22–end Phil. 3. 1–14	(Ps. 119. 41–56) Ecclus. 39. 1–10 *or* Isa. 56. 1–8 Col. 1.24 – 2.7
Ps. *24*; 33 *alt.* Ps. *138*; 140; 141 Hos. 5.8 – 6.6 1 Cor. 11. 2–16	W *or* G	Gen. ch. 15 Matt. 26. 47–56	Hos. 5.8 – 6.6 1 Cor. 11. 2–16
Ps. *67*; 77 *alt.* Ps. 145 Hos. 6.7 – 7.2 1 Cor. 11. 17–end	W *or* G	Gen. ch. 16 Matt. 26. 57–end	Hos. 6.7 – 7.2 1 Cor. 11. 17–end
Ps. *72*; 76 *alt.* Ps. *148*; 149; 150 Hos. ch. 8 1 Cor. 12. 1–11 ct	W *or* G	Gen. 17. 1–22 Matt. 27. 1–10	Hos. ch. 8 1 Cor. 12. 1–11 ct
	THE FOURTH SUNDAY AFTER EPIPHANY		
Ps. 34. 1–10 [11–end] 1 Sam. 3. 1–20 1 Cor. 14. 12–20 *Gospel:* Matt. 13. 10–17	1 Sam. 10. 17–24 Ps. 97 Rom. 13. 1–7 Matt. 8. 23–34 W *or* G	Ps. 71. 1–6, 15–17 Jer. 1. 4–10 Mark 1. 40–end	Ps. 34. 1–10 [11–end] 1 Sam. 3. 1–20 1 Cor. 14. 12–20
Ps. 2; *20*** *alt.* Ps. *4*; 7 Hos. ch. 9 1 Cor. 12. 12–end	**Charles, King and Martyr, 1649** Com. Martyr Wr *or* Gr	Gen. 18. 1–15 Matt. 27. 11–26	Hos. ch. 9 1 Cor. 12. 12–end
Ps. *19*; 21*** *alt.* Ps. *9*; 10† Hos. ch. 10 1 Cor. ch. 13	W *or* G	Gen. 18. 16–end Matt. 27. 27–44	Hos. ch. 10 1 Cor. ch. 13
First EP of The Presentation Ps. 118 1 Sam. 1. 19b–end Heb. 4. 11–end ㊗ ct	W *or* G		*First EP of The Presentation* Ps. 118 1 Sam. 1. 19b–end Heb. 4. 11–end ㊗ ct

February 2006

			Sunday Principal Service / Weekday Eucharist	Third Service / Morning Prayer
2	Th	**THE PRESENTATION OF CHRIST IN THE TEMPLE (CANDLEMAS)**	Mal. 3. 1–5 Ps. 24. [1–6] 7–end Heb. 2. 14–end	*MP:* Ps. *48*; 146 Exod. 13. 1–16 Rom. 12. 1–5
	ꟾ		Luke 2. 22–40	
		or, if The Presentation is observed on 29 January:	1 Kings 2. 1–4, 10–12 Canticle: 1 Chron. 29. 10–12 *or* Ps. 145. 1–5	Ps. 14; *15*; 16 Gen. 21. 1–21 Matt. 27. 57–end
	G		Mark 6. 7–13	
3	F	**Anskar, Archbishop of Hamburg, Missionary in Denmark and Sweden, 865** Ordinary Time starts today (or on 30 January if The Presentation is observed on 29 January) Com. Missionary *or* Ecclus. 47. 2–11 *esp.* Isa. 52. 7–10 Ps. 18. 31–36, 50–end	Ps. 17; *19* Gen. 22. 1–19	
	Gw	*also* Rom. 10. 11–15	Mark 6. 14–29	Matt. 28. 1–15
4	Sa	*Gilbert of Sempringham, Founder of the Gilbertine Order, 1189*	1 Kings 3. 4–13 Ps. 119. 9–16 Mark 6. 30–34	Ps. 20; 21; *23* Gen. ch. 23 Matt. 28. 16–end
	G			
5	S	THE FOURTH SUNDAY BEFORE LENT (Proper 1)	Isa. 40. 21–end Ps. 147. 1–12 [21c] 1 Cor. 9. 16–23	Ps. 2; 3 Jer. 26. 1–16 Acts 3. 1–10
	G		Mark 1. 29–39	
6 DEL 5	M	*The Martyrs of Japan, 1597* (The Accession of Queen Elizabeth II may be observed on 6 February, and Collect, Readings and Post-Communion for the sovereign used.) 1 Kings 8. 1–7, 9–13 Ps. 132. 1–9	Ps. 27; *30* Lev. 19. 1–18, 30–end	
	G		Mark 6. 53–end	1 Tim. 1. 1–17
7	Tu		1 Kings 8. 22–23, 27–30 Ps. 84. 1–10	Ps. 32; *36* Lev. 23. 1–22
	G		Mark 7. 1–13	1 Tim. 1.18 – 2.end
8	W		1 Kings 10. 1–10 Ps. 37. 3–6, 30–32	Ps. 34 Lev. 23. 23–end
	G		Mark 7. 14–23	1 Tim. ch. 3
9	Th		1 Kings 11. 4–13 Ps. 106. 3, 36–42	Ps. 37† Lev. 24. 1–9
	G		Mark 7. 24–30	1 Tim. ch. 4
10	F	*Scholastica, sister of Benedict, Abbess of Plombariola, c. 543*	1 Kings 11. 29–32; 12. 19 Ps. 81. 8–14	Ps. 31 Lev. 25. 1–24
	G		Mark 7. 31–end	1 Tim. 5. 1–16
11	Sa		1 Kings 12. 26–32; 13. 33–end Ps. 106. 6–7, 20–23 Mark 8. 1–10	Ps. 41; *42*; 43 Num. 6. 1–5, 21–end 1 Tim. 5. 17–end
	G			
12	S	THE THIRD SUNDAY BEFORE LENT (Proper 2)	2 Kings 5. 1–14 Ps. 30 1 Cor. 9. 24–end	Ps. 7 Jer. 30. 1–3, 10–22 Acts ch. 6
	G		Mark 1. 40–end	
13 DEL 6	M		James 1. 1–11 Ps. 119. 65–72 Mark 8. 11–13	Ps. 44 Gen. 24. 1–28 1 Tim. 6. 1–10
	G			
14	Tu	**Cyril and Methodius, Missionaries to the Slavs, 869 and 885** *Valentine, Martyr at Rome, c. 269* Com. Missionaries *or* James 1. 12–18 *esp.* Isa. 52. 7–10 Ps. 94. 12–18	Ps. *48*; 52 Gen. 24. 29–end	
	Gw	*also* Rom. 10. 11–15	Mark 8. 14–21	1 Tim. 6. 11–end

Second Service Evening Prayer	Calendar and Holy Communion	Morning Prayer	Evening Prayer
	THE PRESENTATION OF CHRIST IN THE TEMPLE		
EP: Ps. 122; *132*	Mal. 3. 1–5	Ps. 48; 146	Ps. 122; 132
Hag. 2. 1–9	Ps. 48. 1–7	Exod. 13. 1–16	Hag. 2. 1–9
John 2. 18–22	Gal. 4. 1–7	Rom. 12. 1–5	John 2. 18–22
	Luke 2. 22–40		
Ps. 18†			
Hos. 11.12 – 12.end			
1 Cor. 14. 20–end	₩		
	Blasius, Bishop of Sebastopol, Martyr, *c.* 316		
Ps. 22	Com. Martyr	Gen. 22. 1–19	Hos. 13. 1–14
Hos. 13. 1–14		Matt. 28. 1–15	1 Cor. 16. 1–9
1 Cor. 16. 1–9	Gr		
Ps. *24*; 25		Gen. ch. 23	Hos. ch. 14
Hos. ch. 14		Matt. 28. 16–end	1 Cor. 16. 10–end
1 Cor. 16. 10–end			
ct	G		ct
	THE FIFTH SUNDAY AFTER EPIPHANY		
Ps. 5	Hos. 6. 4–6	Ps. 2; 3	Ps. 5
Num. 13. 1–2, 27–end	Ps. 118. 14–21	Jer. 26. 1–16	Num. 13. 1–2, 27–end
Phil. 2. 12–28	Col. 3. 12–17	Acts 3. 1–10	Phil. 2. 12–28
Gospel: Luke 5. 1–11	G Matt. 13. 24b–30		
	The Accession of Queen Elizabeth II, 1952		
	For Accession Service: Ps. 20; 101; 121; Josh. 1. 1–9; Prov. 8. 1–16; Rom. 13. 1–10; Rev. 21.22 – 22.4		
Ps. 26; *28*; 29	*For The Accession:*		
1 Chron. 28. 1–10	1 Pet. 2. 11–17	Lev. 19. 1–18, 30–end	1 Chron. 28. 1–10
John 15. 1–11	G Matt. 22. 16–22	1 Tim. 1. 1–17	John 15. 1–11
Ps. 33		Lev. 23. 1–22	1 Chron. 28. 11–end
1 Chron. 28. 11–end		1 Tim. 1.18 – 2.end	John 15. 12–17
John 15. 12–17	G		
Ps. 119. 33–56		Lev. 23. 23–end	1 Chron. 29. 1–9
1 Chron. 29. 1–9		1 Tim. ch. 3	John 15. 18–end
John 15. 18–end	G		
Ps. 39; *40*		Lev. 24. 1–9	1 Chron. 29. 10–20
1 Chron. 29. 10–20		1 Tim. ch. 4	John 16. 1–15
John 16. 1–15	G		
Ps. 35		Lev. 25. 1–24	1 Chron. 29. 21–end
1 Chron. 29. 21–end		1 Tim. 5. 1–16	John 16. 16–22
John 16. 16–22	G		
Ps. 45; *46*		Num. 6. 1–5, 21–end	2 Chron. 1. 1–13
2 Chron. 1. 1–13		1 Tim. 5. 17–end	John 16. 23–end
John 16. 23–end			
ct	G		ct
	SEPTUAGESIMA		
Ps. 6	Gen. 1. 1–5	Ps. 7	Ps. 6
Num. 20. 2–13	Ps. 9. 10–20	Jer. 30. 1–3, 10–22	Num. 20. 2–13
Phil. 3. 7–end	1 Cor. 9. 24–end	Acts ch. 6	Phil. 3. 7–end
Gospel: Luke 6. 17–26	G Matt. 20. 1–16		
Ps. *47*; 49		Gen. 24. 1–28	2 Chron. 2. 1–16
2 Chron. 2. 1–16		1 Tim. 6. 1–10	John 17. 1–5
John 17. 1–5			
	G		
	Valentine, Martyr at Rome, *c.* 269		
Ps. 50	Com. Martyr	Gen. 24. 29–end	2 Chron. ch. 3
2 Chron. ch. 3		1 Tim. 6. 11–end	John 17. 6–19
John 17. 6–19	Gr		

February 2006

	Sunday Principal Service / Weekday Eucharist	Third Service / Morning Prayer

15 W

Sigfrid, Bishop, Apostle of Sweden, 1045; Thomas Bray, Priest, Founder of the SPCK and the SPG, 1730

	James 1. 19– end	Ps. 119. 57–80
	Ps. 15	Gen. 25. 7–11, 19–end
G	Mark 8. 22–26	2 Tim. 1. 1–14

16 Th

	James 2. 1–9	Ps. 56; 57 (63†)
	Ps. 34. 1–7	Gen. 26.34 – 27.40
G	Mark 8. 27–33	2 Tim. 1.15 – 2.13

17 F

Janani Luwum, Archbishop of Uganda, Martyr, 1977

Com. Martyr *or*	James 2. 14–24, 26	Ps. *51*; 54
also Ecclus. 4. 20–28	Ps. 112	Gen. 27.41 – 28.end
Gr John 12. 24–32	Mark 8.34 – 9.1	2 Tim. 2. 14–end

18 Sa

	James 3. 1–10	Ps. 68
	Ps. 12. 1–7	Gen. 29. 1–30
G	Mark 9. 2–13	2 Tim. ch. 3

19 S

THE SECOND SUNDAY BEFORE LENT

	Prov. 8. 1, 22–31	Ps. 29; 67
	Ps. 104. 26–end	Deut. 8. 1–10
	Col. 1. 15–20	Matt. 6. 25–end
G	John 1. 1–14	

20 M   DEL 7

	James 3. 13–end	Ps. 71
	Ps. 19. 7–end	Gen. 29.31 – 30.24
G	Mark 9. 14–29	2 Tim. 4. 1–8

21 Tu

	James 4. 1–10	Ps. 73
	Ps. 55. 7–9, 24	Gen. 31. 1–24
G	Mark 9. 30–37	2 Tim. 4. 9–end

22 W

	James 4. 13–end	Ps. 77
	Ps. 49. 1–2, 5–10	Gen. 31.25 – 32.2
G	Mark 9. 38–40	Titus ch. 1

23 Th

Polycarp, Bishop of Smyrna, Martyr, c. 155

Com. Martyr *or*	James 5. 1–6	Ps. 78. 1–39†
also Rev. 2. 8–11	Ps. 49. 13–20	Gen. 32. 3–30
	Mark 9. 41–end	Titus ch. 2

Gr

24 F*

	James 5. 9–12	Ps. 55
	Ps. 103. 1–4, 8–13	Gen. 33. 1–17
G	Mark 10. 1–12	Titus ch. 3

25 Sa

	James 5. 13–end	Ps. 76; 79
	Ps. 141. 1–4	Gen. ch. 35
G	Mark 10. 13–16	Philemon

26 S

THE SUNDAY NEXT BEFORE LENT

	2 Kings 2. 1–12	Ps. 27; 150
	Ps. 50. 1–6	Exod. 24. 12–end
	2 Cor. 4. 3–6	2 Cor. 3. 12–end
G	Mark 9. 2–9	

27 M   DEL 8

George Herbert, Priest, Poet, 1633

Com. Pastor *or*	1 Pet. 1. 3–9	Ps. *80*; 82
esp. Mal. 2. 5–7	Ps. 111	Gen. 37. 1–11
Matt. 11. 25–30	Mark 10. 17–27	Gal. ch. 1
Gw *also* Rev. 19. 5–9		

28 Tu

	1 Pet. 1. 10–16	Ps. 87; *89. 1–18*
	Ps. 98. 1–5	Gen. 37. 12–end
G	Mark 10. 28–31	Gal. 2. 1–10

*Matthias may be celebrated on 24 February instead of 14 May.

Second Service Evening Prayer		Calendar and Holy Communion	Morning Prayer	Evening Prayer
Ps. *59*; 60 (67) 2 Chron. ch. 5 John 17. 20–end	G		Gen. 25. 7–11, 19–end 2 Tim. 1. 1–14	2 Chron. ch. 5 John 17. 20–end
Ps. 61; *62*; 64 2 Chron. 6. 1–21 John 18. 1–11	G		Gen. 26.34 – 27.40 2 Tim. 1.15 – 2.13	2 Chron. 6. 1–21 John 18. 1–11
Ps. 38 2 Chron. 6. 22–end John 18. 12–27	G		Gen. 27.41 – 28.end 2 Tim. 2. 14–end	2 Chron. 6. 22–end John 18. 12–27
Ps. 65; *66* 2 Chron. ch. 7 John 18. 28–end ct	G		Gen. 29. 1–30 2 Tim. ch. 3	2 Chron. ch. 7 John 18. 28–end
Ps. 65 Gen. 2. 4b–end Luke 8. 22–35	G	**SEXAGESIMA** Gen. 3. 9–19 Ps. 83. 1–2, 13–end 2 Cor. 11. 19–31 Luke 8. 4–15	Ps. 41 Deut. 8. 1–10 Matt. 6. 25–end	Ps. 65 Gen. 2. 4b–end Luke 8. 22–35
Ps. *72*; 75 2 Chron. 9. 1–12 John 19. 1–16	G		Gen. 29.31 – 30.24 2 Tim. 4. 1–8	2 Chron. 9. 1–12 John 19. 1–16
Ps. 74 2 Chron. 10.1 – 11.4 John 19. 17–30	G		Gen. 31. 1–24 2 Tim. 4. 9–end	2 Chron. 10.1 – 11.4 John 19. 17–30
Ps. 119. 81–104 2 Chron. ch. 12 John 19. 31–end	G		Gen. 31.25 – 32.2 Titus ch. 1	2 Chron. ch. 12 John 19. 31–end
Ps. 78. 40–end† 2 Chron. 13.1 – 14.1 John 20. 1–10	G		Gen. 32. 3–30 Titus ch. 2	2 Chron. 13.1 – 14.1 John 20. 1–10 *or First EP of Matthias* (Ps. 147) Isa. 22. 15–22 Phil. 3.13b – 4.1 R ct
Ps. 69 2 Chron. 14. 2–end John 20. 11–18	R	**MATTHIAS THE APOSTLE** 1 Sam. 2. 27–35 Ps. 16. 1–7 Acts 1. 15–end Matt. 11. 25–end	(Ps. 15) Jonah 1. 1–9 Acts 2. 37–end	(Ps. 80) 1 Sam. 16. 1–13a Matt. 7. 15–27
Ps. 81; *84* 2 Chron. 15. 1–15 John 20. 19–end ct	G		Gen. ch. 35 Philemon	2 Chron. 15. 1–15 John 20. 19–end ct
Ps. 2 [99] 1 Kings 19. 1–16 2 Pet. 1. 16–end *Gospel:* Mark 9. [2–8] 9–13	G	**QUINQUAGESIMA** Gen. 9. 8–17 Ps. 77. 11–20 1 Cor. ch. 13 Luke 18. 31–43	Ps. 27; 150 Exod. 24. 12–end 2 Cor. 3. 12–end	Ps. 2 [99] 1 Kings 19. 1–16 2 Pet. 1. 16–end
Ps. *85*; 86 Jer. ch. 1 John 3. 1–21	G		Gen. 37. 1–11 Gal. ch. 1	Jer. ch. 1 John 3. 1–21
Ps. 89. 19–end Jer. 2. 1–13 John 3. 22–end	G		Gen. 37. 12–end Gal. 2. 1–10	Jer. 2. 1–13 John 3. 22–end

March 2006

		Sunday Principal Service Weekday Eucharist	Third Service Morning Prayer

1 W   **ASH WEDNESDAY**

Joel 2. 1–2, 12–17
or Isa. 58. 1–12
Ps. 51. 1–18
2 Cor. 5.20b – 6.10
Matt. 6. 1–6, 16–21
P   or John 8. 1–11

MP: Ps. 38
Dan. 9. 3–6, 17–19
1 Tim. 6. 6–19

2 Th   **Chad, Bishop of Lichfield, Missionary, 672***
Com. Missionary   *or*   Deut. 30. 15–end
also 1 Tim. 6. 11b–16   Ps. 1
Pw   Luke 9. 22–25

Ps. 77
alt. Ps. 90; *92*
Gen. ch. 39
Gal. 2. 11–end

3 F

Isa. 58. 1–9a
Ps. 51. 1–5, 17–18
P   Matt. 9. 14–15

Ps. *3*; 7
alt. Ps. *88* (95)
Gen. ch. 40
Gal. 3. 1–14

4 Sa

Isa. 58. 9b–end
Ps. 86. 1–7
P   Luke 5. 27–32

Ps. 71
alt. Ps. 96; *97*; 100
Gen. 41. 1–24
Gal. 3. 15–22

5 S   THE FIRST SUNDAY OF LENT

Gen. 9. 8–17
Ps. 25. 1–9
1 Pet. 3. 18–end
P   Mark 1. 9–15

Ps. 77
Exod. 34. 1–10
Rom. 10. 8b–13

6 M

Lev. 19. 1–2, 11–18
Ps. 19. 7–end
P   Matt. 25. 31–end

Ps. 10; *11*
alt. Ps. *98*; 99; 101
Gen. 41. 25–45
Gal. 3.23 – 4.7

7 Tu   **Perpetua, Felicity and their Companions, Martyrs at Carthage, 203**
Com. Martyr   *or*   Isa. 55. 10–11
esp. Rev. 12. 10–12a   Ps. 34. 4–6, 21–22
also Wisd. 3. 1–7   Matt. 6. 7–15
Pr

Ps. 44
alt. Ps. 106† (*or* 103)
Gen. 41.46 – 42.5
Gal. 4. 8–20

8 W   **Edward King, Bishop of Lincoln, 1910**
Ember Day**
Felix, Bishop, Apostle to the East Angles, 647; Geoffrey Studdert Kennedy, Priest, Poet, 1929
Com. Bishop   *or*   Jonah ch. 3
also Heb. 13. 1–8   Ps. 51. 1–5, 17–18
Pw   Luke 11. 29–32

Ps. *6*; 17
alt. Ps. 110; *111*; 112
Gen. 42. 6–17
Gal. 4.21 – 5.1

9 Th

Esther 14. 1–5, 12–14
or Isa. 55. 6–9
Ps. 138
P   Matt. 7. 7–12

Ps. *42*; 43
alt. Ps. 113; *115*
Gen. 42. 18–28
Gal. 5. 2–15

10 F   Ember Day**

Ezek. 18. 21–28
Ps. 130
P   Matt. 5. 20–26

Ps. 22
alt. Ps. 139
Gen. 42. 29–end
Gal. 5. 16–end

11 Sa   Ember Day**

Deut. 26. 16–end
Ps. 119. 1–8
P   Matt. 5. 43–end

Ps. 59; *63*
alt. Ps. 120; *121*; 122
Gen. 43. 1–15
Gal. ch. 6

*Chad may be celebrated with Cedd on 26 October instead of 20 March.
**For Ember Day provision, see p. 13.

Second Service Evening Prayer		Calendar and Holy Communion	Morning Prayer	Evening Prayer
EP: Ps. *51 or* Ps. 102. 1–18 [19–end] Isa. 1. 10–18 Luke 15. 11–end		**ASH WEDNESDAY** Ash Wed. Coll. until 15 April Ps. 38 Commination Joel 2. 12–17 Ps. 57 James 4. 1–10 **P** Matt. 6. 16–21	Dan. 9. 3–6, 17–19 1 Tim. 6. 6–19	Ps. *51 or* Ps. 102. 1–18 [19–end] Isa. 1. 10–18 Luke 15. 11–end
Ps. 74 *alt.* Ps. 94 Jer. 2. 14–32 John 4. 1–26	**Pw**	**Chad, Bishop of Lichfield, Missionary, 672** Com. Bishop *or* Exod. 24. 12–end Matt. 8. 5–13	Gen. ch. 39 Gal. 2. 11–end	Jer. 2. 14–32 John 4. 1–26
Ps. 31 *alt.* Ps. 102 Jer. 3. 6–22 John 4. 27–42	**P**	1 Kings 19. 3b–8 Matt. 5.43 – 6.6	Gen. ch. 40 Gal. 3. 1–14	Jer. 3. 6–22 John 4. 27–42
Ps. 73 *alt.* Ps. 104 Jer. 4. 1–18 John 4. 43–end ct	**P**	Isa. 38. 1–6a Mark 6. 45–end	Gen. 41. 1–24 Gal. 3. 15–22	*alt.* Ps. 104 Jer. 4. 1–18 John 4. 43–end ct
Ps. 119. 17–32 Gen. 2. 15–17; 3. 1–7 Rom. 5. 12–19 *or* Luke 13. 31–end	**P**	**THE FIRST SUNDAY IN LENT** Coll. (1) Lent 1 (2) Ash Wednesday Ember until 11th Gen. 3. 1–6 Ps. 91. 1–12 2 Cor. 6. 1–10 Matt. 4. 1–11	Ps. 77 Exod. 34. 1–10 Rom. 10. 8b–13	Ps. 119. 17–32 Gen. 2. 15–17; 3. 1–7 Rom. 5. 12–19 or Luke 13. 31–end
Ps. 12; *13*; 14 *alt.* Ps. *105*† (*or* 103) Jer. 4. 19–end John 5. 1–18	**P**	Ezek. 34. 11–16a Matt. 25. 31–end	Gen. 41. 25–45 Gal. 3.23 – 4.7	Jer. 4. 19–end John 5. 1–18
Ps. 46; *49* *alt.* Ps. 107† Jer. 5. 1–19 John 5. 19–29	**Pr**	**Perpetua, Martyr at Carthage, 203** Com. Martyr *or* Isa. 55. 6–11 Matt. 21. 10–16	Gen. 41.46 – 42.5 Gal. 4. 8–20	Jer. 5. 1–19 John 5. 19–29
Ps. 9; *28* *alt.* Ps. 119. 129–152 Jer. 5. 20–end John 5. 30–end	**P**	Ember Day Ember CEG *or* Isa. 58. 1–9a Matt. 12. 38–end	Gen. 42. 6–17 Gal. 4.21 – 5.1	Jer. 5. 20–end John 5. 30–end
Ps. 137; 138; *142* *alt.* Ps. 114; *116*; 117 Jer. 6. 9–21 John 6. 1–15	**P**	Isa. 58. 9b–end John 8. 31–45	Gen. 42. 18–28 Gal. 5. 2–15	Jer. 6. 9–21 John 6. 1–15
Ps. 54; *55* *alt.* Ps. *130*; 131; 137 Jer. 6. 22–end John 6. 16–27	**P**	Ember Day Ember CEG *or* Ezek. 18. 20–25 John 5. 2–15	Gen. 42. 29–end Gal. 5. 16–end	Jer. 6. 22–end John 6. 16–27
Ps. *4*; 16 *alt.* Ps. 118 Jer. 7. 1–20 John 6. 27–40 ct	**P**	Ember Day Ember CEG *or* Ezek. 18. 26–end Matt. 17. 1–9 *or* Luke 4. 16–21 *or* John 10. 1–16	Gen. 43. 1–15 Gal. ch. 6	Jer. 7. 1–20 John 6. 27–40 ct

March 2006

		Sunday Principal Service Weekday Eucharist	Third Service Morning Prayer

12 S — THE SECOND SUNDAY OF LENT
		Gen. 17. 1–7, 15–16	Ps. 105. 1–6, 37–end
		Ps. 22. 23–end	Isa. 51. 1–11
		Rom. 4. 13–end	Gal. 3. 1–9, 23–end
P		Mark 8. 31–end	

13 M
		Dan. 9. 4–10	Ps. 26; *32*
		Ps. 79. 8–9, 12, 14	*alt.* Ps. 123; 124; 125; *126*
		Luke 6. 36–38	Gen. 43. 16–end
P			Heb. ch. 1

14 Tu
		Isa. 1. 10, 16–20	Ps. 50
		Ps. 50. 8, 16–end	*alt.* Ps. *132*; 133
		Matt. 23. 1–12	Gen. 44. 1–17
P			Heb. 2. 11–end

15 W
		Jer. 18. 18–20	Ps. 35
		Ps. 31. 4–5, 14–18	*alt.* Ps. 119. 153–end
		Matt. 20. 17–28	Gen. 44. 18–end
P			Heb. 2. 10–end

16 Th
		Jer. 17. 5–10	Ps. 34
		Ps. 1	*alt.* Ps. *143*; 146
		Luke 16. 19–end	Gen. 45. 1–15
P			Heb. 3. 1–6

17 F — **Patrick, Bishop, Missionary, Patron of Ireland, *c*. 460**
	Com. Missionary	*or* Gen. 37. 3–4, 12–13, 17–28	Ps. 40; *41*
	also Ps. 91. 1–4, 13–end	Ps. 105. 16–22	*alt.* Ps. 142; *144*
	Luke 10. 1–12, 17–20	Matt. 21. 33–43, 45–46	Gen. 45. 16–end
Pw			Heb. 3. 7–end

18 Sa — *Cyril, Bishop of Jerusalem, Teacher, 386*
		Mic. 7. 4–15, 18–20	Ps. 3; *25*
		Ps. 103. 1–4, 9–12	*alt.* Ps. 147
		Luke 15. 1–3, 11–end	Gen. 46. 1–7, 28–end
			Heb. 4. 1–13
P			

19 S — THE THIRD SUNDAY OF LENT
		Exod. 20. 1–17	Ps. 18. 1–25
		Ps. 19. [1–6] 7–end	Jer. ch. 38
		1 Cor. 1. 18–25	Phil. 1. 1–26
		John 2. 13–22	
P			

20 M* — JOSEPH OF NAZARETH (transferred from 19 March)**
		2 Sam. 7. 4–16	*MP:* Ps. 25; 147. 1–12
		Ps. 89. 27–36	Isa. 11. 1–10
		Rom. 4. 13–18	Matt. 13. 54–end
W		Matt. 1. 18–end	

21 Tu — **Thomas Cranmer, Archbishop of Canterbury, Reformation Martyr, 1556**
	Com. Martyr	*or* Song of the Three 2, 11–20	Ps. 6; *9*
		or Dan. 2. 20–23	*alt.* Ps. *5*; 6; (8)
		Ps. 25. 3–10	Gen. 47.28 – 48.end
Pr		Matt. 18. 21–25	Heb. 5.11 – 6.12

22 W
		Deut. 4. 1, 5–9	Ps. 38
		Ps. 147. 13–end	*alt.* Ps. 119. 1–32
		Matt. 5. 17–19	Gen. 49. 1–32
P			Heb. 6. 13–end

23 Th
		Jer. 7. 23–28	Ps. *56*; 57
		Ps. 95, 1–2, 6–end	*alt.* Ps. 14; *15*; 16
		Luke 11. 14–23	Gen. 49.33 – 50.end
P			Heb. 7. 1–10

*The following readings may replace those provided for Holy Communion on any day (except Joseph of Nazareth and The Annunciation) during the Third Week of Lent, especially in Years B and C when the Gospel of the Samaritan woman is not read on The Third Sunday of Lent: Exod. 17. 1–7; Ps. 95. 1–2, 6–end; John 4. 5–42.

**Cuthbert may be celebrated on 4 September instead of 20 March.

Second Service Evening Prayer	Calendar and Holy Communion		Morning Prayer	Evening Prayer
	THE SECOND SUNDAY IN LENT			
Ps. 135. 1–14 [15–end]	Jer. 17. 5–10		Ps. 105. 1–6, 37–end	Ps. 135. 1–14
Gen. 12. 1–9	Ps. 25. 13–end		Isa. 51. 1–11	[15–end]
Heb. 11. 1–3, 8–16	1 Thess. 4. 1–8		Gal. 3. 1–9, 23–end	Gen. 12. 1–9
Gospel: John 8. 51–end	Matt. 5. 21–28	P		Heb. 11. 1–3, 8–16
Ps. 70; *74*	Heb. 2. 1–10		Gen. 43. 16–end	Jer. 7. 21–end
alt. Ps. *127*; 128; 129	John 8. 21–30		Heb. ch. 1	John 6. 41–51
Jer. 7. 21–end				
John 6. 41–51		P		
Ps. *52*; 53; 54	Heb. 2. 11–end		Gen. 44. 1–17	Jer. 8. 1–15
alt. Ps. (134) *135*	Matt. 23. 1–12		Heb. 2. 11–end	John 6. 52–59
Jer. 8. 1–15				
John 6. 52–59		P		
Ps. *3*; 51	Heb. 3. 1–6		Gen. 44. 18–end	Jer. 8.18 – 9.11
alt. Ps. 136	Matt. 20. 17–28		Heb. 2. 10–end	John 6. 60–end
Jer. 8.18 – 9.11				
John 6. 60–end		P		
Ps. 71	Heb. 3. 7–end		Gen. 45. 1–15	Jer. 9. 12–24
alt. Ps. *138*; 140; 141	John 5. 30–end		Heb. 3. 1–6	John 7. 1–13
Jer. 9. 12–24				
John 7. 1–13		P		
Ps. *6*; 38	Heb. ch. 4		Gen. 45. 16–end	Jer. 10. 1–16
alt. Ps. 145	Matt. 21. 33–end		Heb. 3. 7–end	John 7. 14–24
Jer. 10. 1–16				
John 7. 14–24		P		
	Edward, King of W. Saxons, 978			
Ps. *23*; 27	Com. Martyr *or*		Gen. 46. 1–7, 28–end	Jer. 10. 17–24
alt. Ps. *148*; 149; 150	Heb. ch. 5		Heb. 4. 1–13	John 7. 25–36
Jer. 10. 17–24	Luke 15. 11–end			
John 7. 25–36				
ct		Pr		ct
	THE THIRD SUNDAY IN LENT			
Ps. 11; 12	Num. 22. 21–31		Ps. 18. 1–25	Ps. 11; 12
Exod. 5.1 – 6.1	Ps. 9. 13–end		Jer. ch. 38	Exod. 5.1 – 6.1
Phil. 3. 4b–14	Eph. 5. 1–14		Phil. 1. 1–26	Phil. 3. 4b–14
or Matt. 10. 16–22	Luke 11. 14–28			*or* Matt. 10. 16–22
or First EP of Joseph				
Ps. 132				
Hos. 11. 1–9				
Luke 2. 41–end				
W ct		P		
	To celebrate Joseph, see *Common Worship* provision.			
EP: Ps. 1; 112	Heb. 6. 1–10		Gen. 47. 1–27	Jer. 11. 1–17
Gen. 50. 22–end	Luke 4. 23–30		Heb. 4.14 – 5.10	John 7. 37–52
Matt. 2. 13–end				
		P		
	Benedict, Abbot of Monte Cassino, c. 550			
Ps. 61; 62; *64*	Com. Abbot *or*		Gen. 47.28 – 48.end	Jer. 11.18 – 12.6
alt. Ps. *9*; 10†	Heb. 6. 11–end		Heb. 5.11 – 6.12	John 7.53 – 8.11
Jer. 11.18 – 12.6	Matt. 18. 15–22			
John 7.53 – 8.11		Pw		
Ps. 36; *39*	Heb. 7. 1–10		Gen. 49. 1–32	Jer. 13. 1–11
alt. Ps. *11*; 12; 13	Matt. 15. 1–20		Heb. 6. 13–end	John 8. 12–30
Jer. 13. 1–11				
John 8. 12–30		P		
Ps. *59*; 60	Heb. 7. 11–25		Gen. 49.33 – 50.end	Jer. ch. 14
alt. Ps. 18†	John 6. 26–35		Heb. 7. 1–10	John 8. 31–47
Jer. ch. 14				
John 8. 31–47		P		

March 2006

	Sunday Principal Service / Weekday Eucharist	Third Service / Morning Prayer

24 F — *Walter Hilton of Thurgarton, Augustinian Canon, Mystic, 1396; Oscar Romero, Archbishop of San Salvador, Martyr, 1980*

Hos. 14. 2–10	Ps. 22
Ps. 81. 6–10, 13, 16	*alt.* Ps. 17; *19*
Mark 12. 28–34	Exod. 1. 1–14
	Heb. 7. 11–end

P

25 Sa — **THE ANNUNCIATION OF OUR LORD TO THE BLESSED VIRGIN MARY**

Isa. 7. 10–14	*MP:* Ps. 111; 113
Ps. 40. 5–10	1 Sam. 2. 1–10
Heb. 10. 4–10	Rom. 5. 12–end
⅏ Luke 1. 26–38	

26 S — THE FOURTH SUNDAY OF LENT
(Mothering Sunday)

Num. 21. 4–9	Ps. 27
Ps. 107. 1–3, 17–22	1 Sam 16. 1–13
(*or* 107. 1–9)	John 9. 1–25
Eph. 2. 1–10	
John 3. 14–21	

or, for Mothering Sunday:

Exod. 2. 1–10
or 1 Sam. 1. 20–end
Ps. 34. 11–20
or Ps. 127. 1–4
2 Cor. 1. 3–7
or Col. 3. 12–17
Luke 2. 33–35
or John 19. 25b–27

P

27 M*

Isa. 65. 17–21	Ps. 70; 77
Ps. 30. 1–5, 8, 11–end	*alt.* Ps. 27; *30*
John 4. 43–end	Exod. 2. 11–22
	Heb. 9. 1–14

P

28 Tu

Ezek. 47. 1–9, 12	Ps. 54; *79*
Ps. 46. 1–8	*alt.* Ps. 32; *36*
John 5. 1–3, 5–16	Exod. 2.23 – 3.20
	Heb. 9. 15–end

P

29 W

Isa. 49. 8–15	Ps. 63; *90*
Ps. 145. 8–17	*alt.* Ps. 34
John 5. 17–30	Exod. 4. 1–23
	Heb. 10. 1–18

P

30 Th

Exod. 32. 7–14	Ps. 53; *86*
Ps. 106. 19–23	*alt.* Ps. 37†
John 5. 31–47	Exod. 4.27 – 6.1
	Heb. 10. 19–25

31 F — *John Donne, Priest, Poet, 1631*

Wisd. 2. 1, 12–22	Ps. 102
or Jer. 26. 8–11	*alt.* Ps. 31
Ps. 34. 15–end	Exod. 6. 2–13
John 7. 1–2, 10, 25–30	Heb. 10. 26–end

P

April 2006

1 Sa — *Frederick Denison Maurice, Priest, Teacher, 1872*

Jer. 11. 18–20	Ps. 32
Ps. 7. 1–2, 8–10	*alt.* Ps. 41; *42*; 43
John 7. 40–52	Exod. 7. 8–end
	Heb. 11. 1–16

P

*The following readings may replace those provided for Holy Communion on any day during the Fourth Week of Lent, especially in Years B and C when the Gospel of the man born blind is not read on The Fourth Sunday of Lent: Mic. 7. 7–9; Ps. 27. 1, 9–10, 16–17; John ch. 9.

Second Service Evening Prayer		Calendar and Holy Communion	Morning Prayer	Evening Prayer
First EP of The Annunciation Ps. 85 Wisd. 9. 1–12 *or* Gen. 3. 8–15 Gal. 4. 1–5		Heb. 7. 26–end John 4. 5–26	Exod. 1. 1–14 Heb. 7. 11–end	*First EP of The* *Annunciation* Ps. 85 Wisd. 9. 1–12 *or* Gen. 3. 8–15 Gal. 4. 1–5
℣ ct	P			℣ ct

THE ANNUNCIATION OF THE BLESSED VIRGIN MARY

EP: Ps. 131; 146 Isa. 52. 1–12 Heb. 2. 5–end	 ℣	Isa. 7. 10–14 [15] Ps. 113 Rom. 5. 12–19 Luke 1. 26–38	Ps. 111 1 Sam. 2. 1–10 Heb. 10. 4–10	Ps. 131; 146 Isa. 52. 1–12 Heb. 2. 5–end

THE FOURTH SUNDAY IN LENT
To celebrate Mothering Sunday, see *Common Worship* provision.

Ps. 13; 14 Exod. 6. 2–13 Rom. 5. 1–11 *Gospel:* John 12. 1–8 *If the Principal Service* *readings for The Fourth* *Sunday of Lent are displaced* *by Mothering Sunday* *provisions, they may be used* *at the Second Service.*		Exod. 16. 2–7a Ps. 122 Gal. 4. 21–end *or* Heb. 12. 22–24 John 6. 1–14	Ps. 27 1 Sam 16. 1–13 John 9. 1–25	Ps. 13; 14 Exod. 6. 2–13 Rom. 5. 1–11
	P			
Ps. *25*; 28 *alt.* Ps. 26; *28*; 29 Jer. 17. 5–18 John 9. 18–end	 P	Heb. 11. 1–6 John 2. 13–end	Exod. 2. 11–22 Heb. 9. 1–14	Jer. 17. 5–18 John 9. 18–end
Ps. *80*; 82 *alt.* Ps. 33 Jer. 18. 1–12 John 10. 1–10	 P	Heb. 11. 13–16a John 7. 14–24	Exod. 2.23 – 3.20 Heb. 9. 15–end	Jer. 18. 1–12 John 10. 1–10
Ps. 52; *91* *alt.* Ps. 119. 33–56 Jer. 18. 13–end John 10. 11–21	 P	Heb. 12. 1–11 John 9. 1–17	Exod. 4. 1–23 Heb. 10. 1–18	Jer. 18. 13–end John 10. 11–21
Ps. 94 *alt.* Ps. 39; *40* Jer. 19. 1–13 John 10. 22–end	 P	Heb. 12. 12–17 John 5. 17–27	Exod. 4.27 – 6.1 Heb. 10. 19–25	Jer. 19. 1–13 John 10. 22–end
Ps. 13; *16* *alt.* Ps. 35 Jer. 19.14 – 20.6 John 11. 1–16	 P	Heb. 12. 22–end John 11. 33–46	Exod. 6. 2–13 Heb. 10. 26–end	Jer. 19.14 – 20.6 John 11. 1–16
Ps. *140*; 141; 142 *alt.* Ps. 45; *46* Jer. 20. 7–end John 11. 17–27 ct	 P	Heb. 13. 7–21 John 8. 12–20	Exod. 7. 8–end Heb. 11. 1–16	Jer. 20. 7–end John 11. 17–27 ct

April 2006

		Sunday Principal Service Weekday Eucharist	Third Service Morning Prayer

2 S   THE FIFTH SUNDAY OF LENT (Passiontide begins)

Jer. 31. 31–34
Ps. 51. 1–13
or Ps. 119. 9–16
Heb. 5. 5–10

Ps. 107. 1–22
Exod. 24. 3–8
Heb. 12. 18–end

P   John 12. 20–33

3 M*

Susanna 1–9, 15–17, 19–30,
33–62 (*or* 41b–62)
or Josh. 2. 1–14
Ps. 23

Ps. *73*; 121
alt. Ps. 44
Exod. 8. 1–19
Heb. 11. 17–31

P   John 8. 1–11

4 Tu

Num. 21. 4–9
Ps. 102. 1–3, 16–23
John 8. 21–30

Ps. *35*; 123
alt. Ps. *48*; 52
Exod. 8. 20–end

P   Heb. 11.32 – 12.2

5 W

Dan. 3. 14–20, 24–25, 28
Canticle: Bless the Lord
John 8. 31–42

Ps. *55*; 124
alt. Ps. 119. 57–80
Exod. 9. 1–12

P   Heb. 12. 3–13

6 Th

Gen. 17. 3–9
Ps. 105. 4–9
John 8. 51–end

Ps. *40*; 125
alt. Ps. 56; *57* (63†)
Exod. 9. 13–end

P   Heb. 12. 14–end

7 F

Jer. 20. 10–13
Ps. 18. 1–6
John 10. 31–end

Ps. *22*; 126
alt. Ps. *51*; 54
Exod. ch. 10

P   Heb. 13. 1–16

8 Sa

Ezek. 37. 21–28
Canticle: Jer. 31. 10–13
or Ps. 121
John 11. 45–end

Ps. *23*; 127
alt. Ps. 68
Exod. ch. 11

P   Heb. 13. 17–end

9 S   PALM SUNDAY

Liturgy of the Palms
Mark 11. 1–11
or John 12. 12–16
Ps. 118. [1–2]19–24

Liturgy of the Passion
Isa. 50. 4–9a
Ps. 31. 9–16 [17–18]
Phil. 2. 5–11
Mark 14.1 – 15.end
or Mark 15. 1–39 [40–end]

Ps. 61; 62
Zech. 9. 9–12
1 Cor. 2. 1–12

R

10 M   MONDAY OF HOLY WEEK

Isa. 42. 1–9
Ps. 36. 5–11
Heb. 9. 11–15
John 12. 1–11

Ps. 41
Lam. 1. 1–12a
Luke 22. 1–23

R

11 Tu   TUESDAY OF HOLY WEEK

Isa. 49. 1–7
Ps. 71. 1–8 [9–14]
1 Cor. 1. 18–31
John 12. 20–36

Ps. 27
Lam. 3. 1–18
Luke 22. [24–38] 39–53

R

12 W   WEDNESDAY OF HOLY WEEK

Isa. 50. 4–9a
Ps. 70
Heb. 12. 1–3
John 13. 21–32

Ps. 102. 1–17 [18–end]
Wisd. 1.16 – 2.1, 12–22
or Jer. 11. 18–20
Luke 22. 54–end

R

*The following readings may replace those provided for Holy Communion on any day during the Fifth Week of Lent, especially in Years B and C when the Gospel of Lazarus is not read on The Fifth Sunday of Lent: 2 Kings 4. 18–21, 32–37; Ps. 17. 1–8, 16; John 11. 1–45.

Second Service Evening Prayer	Calendar and Holy Communion	Morning Prayer	Evening Prayer
	THE FIFTH SUNDAY IN LENT		
Ps. 34. 1–10[11–end]	Exod. 24. 4–8	Ps. 107. 1–22	Ps. 34. 1–10[11–end]
Exod. 7. 8–24	Ps. 143	Jer. 31. 31–34	Exod. 7. 8–24
Rom. 5. 12–end	Heb. 9. 11–15	Heb. 5. 5–10	Rom. 5. 12–end
Gospel: Luke 22. 1–13	John 8. 46–end		
	P		
	Richard, Bishop of Chichester, 1253		
Ps. 26; 27	Com. Bishop or	Exod. 8. 1–19	Jer. 21. 1–10
alt. Ps. 47; 49	Col. 1. 13–23a	Heb. 11. 17–31	John 11. 28–44
Jer. 21. 1–10	John 7. 1–13		
John 11. 28–44			
	Pw		
	Ambrose, Bishop of Milan, 397		
Ps. 61; 64	Com. Doctor or	Exod. 8. 20–end	Jer. 22. 1–5, 13–19
alt. Ps. 50	Col. 2. 8–12	Heb. 11.32 – 12.2	John 11. 45–end
Jer. 22. 1–5, 13–19	John 7. 32–39		
John 11. 45–end	Pw		
Ps. 56; 62	Col. 2. 13–19	Exod. 9. 1–12	Jer. 22.20 – 23.8
alt. Ps. 59; 60 (67)	John 7. 40–end	Heb. 12. 3–13	John 12. 1–11
Jer. 22.20 – 23.8			
John 12. 1–11	P		
Ps. 42; 43	Col. 3. 8–11	Exod. 9. 13–end	Jer. 23. 9–32
alt. Ps. 61; 62; 64	John 10. 22–38	Heb. 12. 14–end	John 12. 12–19
Jer. 23. 9–32			
John 12. 12–19	P		
Ps. 31	Col. 3. 12–17	Exod. ch. 10	Jer. ch. 24
alt. Ps. 38	John 11. 47–54	Heb. 13. 1–16	John 12. 20–36a
Jer. ch. 24			
John 12. 20–36a	P		
Ps. 128; 129; 130	Col. 4. 2–6	Exod. ch. 11	Jer. 25. 1–14
alt. Ps. 65; 66	John 6. 53–end	Heb. 13. 17–end	John 12. 36b–end
Jer. 25. 1–14			
John 12. 36b–end			
ct	P		ct
	PALM SUNDAY		
Ps. 69. 1–20	Zech. 9. 9–12	Ps. 61; 62	Ps. 69. 1–20
Isa. 5. 1–7	Ps. 73. 22–end	Isa. 42. 1–9	Isa. 5. 1–7
Mark 12. 1–12	Phil. 2. 5–11	1 Cor. 2. 1–12	Mark 12. 1–12
	Passion acc. to Matthew		
	Matt. 27. 1–54		
	or Matt. 26.1 – 27.61		
	R or Matt. 21. 1–13		
	MONDAY IN HOLY WEEK		
Ps. 25	Isa. 63. 1–19	Ps. 41	Ps. 25
Lam. 2. 8–19	Ps. 55. 1–8	Lam. 1. 1–12a	Lam. 2. 8–19
Col. 1. 18–23	Gal. 6. 1–11	John 12. 1–11	Col. 1. 18–23
	R Mark ch. 14		
	TUESDAY IN HOLY WEEK		
Ps. 55. 13–24	Isa. 50. 5–11	Ps. 27	Ps. 55. 13–24
Lam. 3. 40–51	Ps. 13	Lam. 3. 1–18	Lam. 3. 40–51
Gal. 6. 11–end	Rom. 5. 6–19	John 12. 20–36	Gal. 6. 11–end
	R Mark 15. 1–39		
	WEDNESDAY IN HOLY WEEK		
Ps. 88	Isa. 49. 1–9a	Ps. 102. 1–17 [18–end]	Ps. 88
Isa. 63. 1–9	Ps. 54	Wisd. 1.16 – 2.1,	Isa. 63. 1–9
Rev. 14.18 – 15.4	Heb. 9. 16–end	12–22	Rev. 14.18 – 15.4
	Luke ch. 22	or Jer. 11. 18–20	
	R	John 13. 21–32	

April 2006

	Sunday Principal Service Weekday Eucharist	Third Service Morning Prayer

13 Th   MAUNDY THURSDAY

	Exod. 12. 1–4 [5–10], 11–14	Ps. 42; 43
	Ps. 116. 1, 10–end (*or* 9–end)	Lev. 16. 2–24
	1 Cor. 11. 23–26	Luke 23. 1–25
	John 13. 1–17, 31b–35	

W (HC) R

14 F   GOOD FRIDAY

	Isa. 52.13 – 53.end	*MP:* Ps. 69
	Ps. 22 (*or* 22. 1–11 *or* 22. 1–21)	Gen. 22. 1–18
	Heb. 10. 16–25	*A part of* John 18 – 19 *if not*
	or Heb. 10. 14–16; 5. 7–9	*read at the Principal Service*
R	John 18.1 – 19.end	*or* Heb. 10. 1–10

15 Sa   EASTER EVE

These readings are for use at services other than the Easter Vigil

	Job 14. 1–14	Ps. 142
	or Lam. 3. 1–9, 19–24	Hos. 6. 1–6
	Ps. 31. 1–4, 15–16 (*or* 1–5)	John 2. 18–22
	1 Pet. 4. 1–8	
	Matt. 27. 57–end	
	or John 19. 38–end	

16 S   EASTER DAY

The following readings and psalms (or canticles) are provided for use at the Easter Vigil. A minimum of three Old Testament readings should be chosen. The reading from Exodus ch. 14 should always be used.	Gen. 1.1 – 2.4a & Ps. 136. 1–9, 23–end Gen. 7. 1–5, 11–18; 8. 6–18; 9. 8–13 & Ps. 46 Gen. 22. 1–18 & Ps. 16 Exod. 14. 10–end; 15. 20–21 & *Canticle:* Exod. 15. 1b–13, 17–18 Isa. 55. 1–11 & *Canticle:* Isa. 12. 2–6 Baruch 3.9–15, 32 – 4.4 & Ps. 19 *or* Prov. 8. 1–8, 19–21; 9. 4b–6 & Ps. 19 Ezek. 36. 24–28 & Ps. 42; 43 Ezek. 37. 1–14 & Ps. 143 Zeph. 3. 14–end & Ps. 98 Rom. 6. 3–11 & Ps. 114 Mark 16. 1–8	
Easter Day Services *The reading from Acts must be used as either the first or second reading at the Principal Service*	Acts 10. 34–43 *or* Isa. 25. 6–9 Ps. 118. [1–2] 14–24 1 Cor. 15. 1–11 *or* Acts 10. 34–43 John 20. 1–18 *or* Mark 16. 1–8	*MP:* Ps. 114; 117 Gen. 1. 1–5, 26–end 2 Cor. 5.14 – 6.2

17 M   MONDAY OF EASTER WEEK

	Acts 2. 14, 22–32	Ps. *111*; 117; 146
	Ps. 16. 1–2, 6–end	Exod. 12. 1–14
	Matt. 28. 8–15	1 Cor. 15. 1–11

W

18 Tu   TUESDAY OF EASTER WEEK

	Acts 2. 36–41	Ps. *112*; 147. 1–12
	Ps. 33. 4–5, 18–end	Exod. 12. 14–36
	John 20. 11–18	1 Cor. 15. 12–19

W

19 W   WEDNESDAY OF EASTER WEEK

	Acts 3. 1–10	Ps. *113*; 147. 13–end
	Ps. 105. 1–9	Exod. 12. 37–end
	Luke 24. 13–35	1 Cor. 15. 20–28

W

20 Th   THURSDAY OF EASTER WEEK

	Acts 3. 11–end	Ps. *114*; 148
	Ps. 8	Exod. 13. 1–16
	Luke 24. 35–48	1 Cor. 15. 29–34

W

Second Service Evening Prayer	Calendar and Holy Communion	Morning Prayer	Evening Prayer
	MAUNDY THURSDAY		
Ps. 39	Exod. 12. 1–11	Ps. 42; 43	Ps. 39
Exod. ch. 11	Ps. 43	Lev. 16. 2–24	Exod. ch. 11
Eph. 2. 11–18	1 Cor. 11. 17–end	John 13. 1–17, 31b–35	Eph. 2. 11–18
	Luke 23. 1–49		
	W (HC) R		
	GOOD FRIDAY		
	Alt. Collect Passion acc. to John		
	Alt. Gospel, if Passion is read		
EP: Ps. 130; 143	Num. 21. 4–9	Ps. 69	Ps. 130; 143
Lam. 5. 15–22	Ps. 140. 1–9	Gen. 22. 1–18	Lam. 5. 15–22
John 19. 38–end	Heb. 10. 1–25	John ch. 18	John 19. 38–end
or Col. 1. 18–23	John 19. 1–37		
	R *or* John 19. 38–end		
	EASTER EVE		
Ps. 116	Job 14. 1–14	Ps. 142	Ps. 116
Job 19. 21–27	1 Pet. 3. 17–22	Hos. 6. 1–6	Job 19. 21–27
1 John 5. 5–12	Matt. 27. 57–end	John 2. 18–22	1 John 5. 5–12
	EASTER DAY		
	Exod. 12. 21–28	Ps. 114; 117	Ps. 105
	Ps. 111	Gen. 1. 1–5, 26–end	Isa. 25. 6–9
	Col. 3. 1–7	2 Cor. 5.14 – 6.2	Luke 24. 13–35
	John 20. 1–10		
EP: Ps. 105			
or Ps. 66. 1–11			
Ezek. 37. 1–14			
Luke 24. 13–35			
	𝔚		
	MONDAY IN EASTER WEEK		
Ps. 135	Easter Anthems	Exod. 12. 1–14	Song of Sol. 1.9 – 2.7
Song of Sol. 1.9 – 2.7	Hos. 6. 1–6	1 Cor. 15. 1–11	Mark 16. 1–8
Mark 16. 1–8	Acts 10. 34–43		
	W Luke 24. 13–35		
	TUESDAY IN EASTER WEEK		
Ps. 136	1 Kings 17. 17–end	Exod. 12. 14–36	Song of Sol. 2. 8–end
Song of Sol. 2. 8–end	Ps. 16. 9–end	1 Cor. 15. 12–19	Luke 24. 1–12
Luke 24. 1–12	Acts 13. 26–41		
	W Luke 24. 36b–48		
	WEDNESDAY IN EASTER WEEK		
Ps. 105	Isa. 42. 10–16	Exod. 12. 37–end	Song of Sol. ch. 3
Song of Sol. ch. 3	Ps. 111	1 Cor. 15. 20–28	Matt. 28. 16–end
Matt. 28. 16–end	Acts 3. 12–18		
	W John 20. 11–18		
	THURSDAY IN EASTER WEEK		
Ps. 106	Isa. 43. 16–21	Exod. 13. 1–16	Song of Sol. 5.2 – 6.3
Song of Sol. 5.2 – 6.3	Ps. 113	1 Cor. 15. 29–34	Luke 7. 11–17
Luke 7. 11–17	Acts 8. 26–end		
	W John 21. 1–14		

April 2006

		Sunday Principal Service Weekday Eucharist	Third Service Morning Prayer

21 F
FRIDAY OF EASTER WEEK

Acts 4. 1–12
Ps. 118. 1–4, 22–26
John 21. 1–14

Ps. *115*; 149
Exod. 13.17 – 14.14
1 Cor. 15. 35–50

W

22 Sa
SATURDAY OF EASTER WEEK

Acts 4. 13–21
Ps. 118. 1–4, 14–21
Mark 16. 9–15

Ps. *116*; 150
Exod. 14. 15–end
1 Cor. 15. 51–end

W

23 S
THE SECOND SUNDAY OF EASTER
(George transferred to 24th)
The reading from Acts must
be used as either the first or
second reading at the
Principal Service

Acts 4. 32–35
[*or* Exod. 14. 10–end; 15. 20–21]
Ps. 133
1 John 1.1 – 2.2
John 20. 19–end

Ps. 22. 20–31
Isa. 53. 6–12
Rom. 4. 13–25

W

24 M
GEORGE, MARTYR, PATRON OF ENGLAND, *C.* **304** (transferred from 23rd)

1 Macc. 2. 59–64
or Rev. 12. 7–12
Ps. 126
2 Tim. 2. 3–13
John 15. 18–21

MP: Ps. 5; 146
Josh. 1. 1–9
Eph. 6. 10–20

R

25 Tu
MARK THE EVANGELIST

Prov. 15. 28–end
or Acts 15. 35–end
Ps. 119. 9–16
Eph. 4. 7–16
Mark 13. 5–13

MP: Ps. 37. 23–41; 148
Isa. 62. 6–10
or Ecclus. 51. 13–end
Acts 12.25 – 13.13

R

26 W

Acts 5. 17–26
Ps. 34. 1–8
John 3. 16–21

Ps. 16; *30*
alt. Ps. 119. 1–32
Exod. 16. 11–end
Col. 2. 1–15

W

27 Th
Christina Rossetti, Poet, 1894

Acts 5. 27–33
Ps. 34. 1, 15–end
John 3. 31–end

Ps. *28*; 29
alt. Ps. 14; *15*; 16
Exod. ch. 17
Col. 2.16 – 3.11

W

28 F
Peter Chanel, Missionary in the South Pacific, Martyr, 1841

Acts 5. 34–42
Ps. 27. 1–5, 16–17
John 6. 1–15

Ps. 57; *61*
alt. Ps. 17; *19*
Exod. 18. 1–12
Col. 3.12 – 4.1

W

29 Sa
Catherine of Siena, Teacher, 1380
Com. Teacher   *or*
also Prov. 8. 1, 6–11
John 17. 12–26

Acts 6. 1–7
Ps. 33. 1–5, 18–19
John 6. 16–21

Ps. 63; *84*
alt. Ps. 20; 21; *23*
Exod. 18. 13–end
Col. 4. 2–end

W

30 S
THE THIRD SUNDAY OF EASTER
The reading from Acts must
be used as either the first or
second reading at the
Principal Service

Acts 3. 12–19
[*or* Zeph. 3. 14–end]
Ps. 4
1 John 3. 1–7
Luke 24. 36b–48

Ps. 77. 11–20
Isa. 63. 7–15
1 Cor. 10. 1–13

W

Second Service Evening Prayer		Calendar and Holy Communion	Morning Prayer	Evening Prayer
		FRIDAY IN EASTER WEEK		
Ps. 107		Ezek. 37. 1–14	Exod. 13.17 – 14.14	Song of Sol. 7.10 – 8.4
Song of Sol. 7.10 – 8.4		Ps. 116. 1–9	1 Cor. 15. 35–50	Luke 8. 41–end
Luke 8. 41–end		1 Pet. 3. 18–end		
	W	Matt. 28. 16–end		
		SATURDAY IN EASTER WEEK		
Ps. 145		Zech. 8. 1–8	Exod. 14. 15–end	Song of Sol. 8. 5–7
Song of Sol. 8. 5–7		Ps. 118. 14–21	1 Cor. 15. 51–end	John 11. 17–44
John 11. 17–44		1 Pet. 2. 1–10		
ct	W	John 20. 24–end		ct
		THE FIRST SUNDAY AFTER EASTER		
Ps. 143. 1–11		Ezek. 37. 1–10	Ps. 22. 20–31	Ps. 143. 1–11
Isa. 26. 1–9, 19		Ps. 81. 1–4	Isa. 53. 6–12	Isa. 26. 1–9, 19
Luke 24. 1–12		1 John 5. 4–12	Rom. 4. 13–25	Luke 24. 1–12
or First EP of George		John 20. 19–23		*or First EP of George*
Ps. 111; 116				(Ps. 111; 116)
Jer. 15.15–end				Jer. 15.15–end
Heb. 11. 32–12.2				Heb. 11. 32–12.2
R ct	W			**R ct**
		George, Martyr, Patron of England, *c.* **304**		
		To celebrate George, see *Common Worship* provision.		
EP: Ps. 3; 11		*Also* Com. Martyr	Exod. 15. 1–21	Deut. 1. 3–18
Isa. 43. 1–7			Col. 1. 1–14	John 20. 1–10
John 15. 1–8				*or First EP of Mark*
or First EP of Mark				(Ps. 19)
Ps. 19				Isa. 52. 7–10
Isa. 52. 7–10				Mark 1. 1–15
Mark 1. 1–15				
R ct	Wr			**R ct**
		MARK THE EVANGELIST		
EP: Ps. 45		Prov. 15. 28–end	(Ps. 37. 23–41; 148)	(Ps. 45)
Ezek. 1. 4–14		Ps. 119. 9–16	Isa. 62. 6–10	Ezek. 1. 4–14
2 Tim. 4. 1–11		Eph. 4. 7–16	*or* Ecclus. 51. 13–end	2 Tim. 4. 1–11
		John 15. 1–11	Acts 12.25 – 13.13	
	R			
Ps. 33			Exod. 16. 11–end	Deut. 3. 18–end
alt. Ps. *11*; 12; 13		-	Col. 2. 1–15	John 20. 19–end
Deut. 3. 18–end				
John 20. 19–end	W			
Ps. 34			Exod. ch. 17	Deut. 4. 1–14
alt. Ps. 18†			Col. 2.16 – 3.11	John 21. 1–14
Deut. 4. 1–14				
John 21. 1–14	W			
Ps. 118			Exod. 18. 1–12	Deut. 4. 15–31
alt. Ps. 22			Col. 3.12 – 4.1	John 21. 15–19
Deut. 4. 15–31				
John 21. 15–19	W			
Ps. 66			Exod. 18. 13–end	Deut. 4. 32–40
alt. Ps. *24*; 25			Col. 4. 2–end	John 21. 20–end
Deut. 4. 32–40				
John 21. 20–end	W			
		THE SECOND SUNDAY AFTER EASTER		
Ps. 142		Ezek. 34. 11–16a	Ps. 77. 11–20	Ps. 142
Deut. 7. 7–13		Ps. 23	Isa. 63. 7–15	Deut. 7. 7–13
Rev. 2. 1–11		1 Pet. 2. 19–25	1 Cor. 10. 1–13	Rev. 2. 1–11
Gospel: Luke 16. 19–end		John 10. 11–16		*or First EP of Philip*
or First EP of Philip				*and James*
and James				(Ps. 119. 1–8)
Ps. 25				Isa. 40. 27–end
Isa. 40. 27–end				John 20. 12–26
John 20. 12–26				
R ct	W			**R ct**

May 2006

	Sunday Principal Service / Weekday Eucharist	Third Service / Morning Prayer

1 M — PHILIP AND JAMES, APOSTLES

Isa. 30. 15–21
Ps. 119. 1–8
Eph. 1. 3–10
John 14. 1–14

MP: Ps. 139; 146
Prov. 4. 10–18
James 1. 1–12

R

2 Tu — Athanasius, Bishop of Alexandria, Teacher, 373
Com. Teacher *or* Acts 7.51 – 8.1
also Ecclus. 4. 20–28 Ps. 31. 1–5, 16
Matt. 10. 24–27 John 6. 30–35

Ps. *98*; 99; 100
alt. Ps. 32; *36*
Exod. 20. 1–21
Luke 1. 26–38

W

3 W

Acts 8. 1b–8
Ps. 66. 1–6
John 6. 35–40

Ps. 105
alt. Ps. 34
Exod. ch. 24
Luke 1. 39–56

W

4 Th — The Saints and Martyrs of the Reformation Era
Isa. 43. 1–7 *or* Acts 8. 26–end
or Ecclus. 2. 10–17 Ps. 66. 7–8, 14–end
Ps. 87 John 6. 44–51
2 Cor. 4. 5–12
John 12. 20–26

Ps. 136
alt. Ps. 37†
Exod. 25. 1–22
Luke 1. 57–end

W

5 F

Acts 9. 1–20
Ps. 117
John 6. 52–59

Ps. 107
alt. Ps. 31
Exod. 28. 1–4a, 29–38
Luke 2. 1–20

W

6 Sa

Acts 9. 31–42
Ps. 116. 10–15
John 6. 60–69

Ps. 108; *110*; 111
alt. Ps. 41; *42*; 43
Exod. 29. 1–9
Luke 2. 21–40

W

7 S — THE FOURTH SUNDAY OF EASTER
The reading from Acts must Acts 4. 5–12
be used as either the first or [Gen. 7. 1–5, 11–18; 8. 6–18;
second reading at the 9. 8–13]
Principal Service Ps. 23
1 John 3. 16–end
John 10. 11–18

Ps. 119. 89–96
Neh. 7.73b – 8.12
Luke 24. 25–32

W

8 M — Julian of Norwich, Spiritual Writer, *c.* 1417
Com. Religious *or* Acts 11. 1–18
also 1 Cor. 13. 8–end Ps. 42. 1–2; 43. 1–4
Matt. 5. 13–16 John 10. 1–10 (*or* 11–18)

Ps. 103
alt. Ps. 44
Exod. 32. 1–14
Luke 2. 41–end

W

9 Tu

Acts 11. 19–26
Ps. 87
John 10. 22–30

Ps. 139
alt. Ps. *48*; 52
Exod. 32. 15–34
Luke 3. 1–14

W

10 W

Acts 12.24 –13.5
Ps. 67
John 12. 44–end

Ps. 135
alt. Ps. 119. 57–80
Exod. ch. 33
Luke 3. 15–22

W

11 Th

Acts 13. 13–25
Ps. 89. 1–2, 20–26
John 13. 16–20

Ps. 118
alt. Ps. 56; *57* (63†)
Exod. 34. 1–10, 27–end
Luke 4. 1–13

W

12 F

Acts 13. 26–33
Ps. 2
John 14. 1–6

Ps. 33
alt. Ps. *51*; 54
Exod. 35.20 – 36.7
Luke 4. 14–30

W

13 Sa

Acts 13. 44–end
Ps. 98. 1–5
John 14. 7–14

Ps. 34
alt. Ps. 68
Exod. 40. 17–end
Luke 4. 31–37

W

Second Service Evening Prayer		Calendar and Holy Communion	Morning Prayer	Evening Prayer
EP: Ps. 149 Job 23. 1–12 John 1. 43–end	**R**	**PHILIP AND JAMES, APOSTLES** Prov. 4. 10–18 Ps. 25. 1–9 James 1. [1]2–12 John 14. 1–14	(Ps. 139; 146) Isa. 30. 1–5 John 12. 20–26	(Ps. 149) Job 23. 1–12 John 1. 43–end
Ps. 71 *alt.* Ps. 33 Deut. 5. 22–end Eph. 1. 15–end	**W**		Exod. 20. 1–21 Luke 1. 26–38	Deut. 5. 22–end Eph. 1. 15–end
Ps. 67; *72* *alt.* Ps. 119. 33–56 Deut. ch. 6 Eph. 2. 1–10	**Wr**	**The Invention of the Cross** Exod. ch. 24 Luke 1. 39–56	Exod. ch. 24 Luke 1. 39–56	Deut. ch. 6 Eph. 2. 1–10
Ps. 73 *alt.* Ps. 39; *40* Deut. 7. 1–11 Eph. 2. 11–end	**W**		Exod. 25. 1–22 Luke 1. 57–end	Deut. 7. 1–11 Eph. 2. 11–end
Ps. 77 *alt.* Ps. 35 Deut. 7. 12–end Eph. 3. 1–13	**W**		Exod. 28. 1–4a, 29–38 Luke 2. 1–20	Deut. 7. 12–end Eph. 3. 1–13
Ps. 23; *27* *alt.* Ps. 45; *46* Deut. ch. 8 Eph. 3. 14–end ct	**W**	**John the Evangelist, ante Portam Latinam** CEG of 27 December	Exod. 29. 1–9 Luke 2. 21–40	Deut. ch. 8 Eph. 3. 14–end ct
Ps. 81. 8–16 Exod. 16. 4–15 Rev. 2. 12–17 *Gospel:* John 6. 30–40	**W**	**THE THIRD SUNDAY AFTER EASTER** Gen. 45. 3–10 Ps. 57 1 Pet. 2. 11–17 John 16. 16–22	Ps. 119. 89–96 Neh. 7.73b – 8.12 Luke 24. 25–32	Ps. 81. 8–16 Exod. 16. 4–15 Rev. 2. 12–17
Ps. 112; 113; *114* *alt.* Ps. *47*; 49 Deut. 9. 1–21 Eph. 4. 1–16	**W**		Exod. 32. 1–14 Luke 2. 41–end	Deut. 9. 1–21 Eph. 4. 1–16
Ps. 115; *116* *alt.* Ps. 50 Deut. 9.23 – 10.5 Eph. 4. 17–end	**W**		Exod. 32. 15–34 Luke 3. 1–14	Deut. 9.23 – 10.5 Eph. 4. 17–end
Ps. *47*; 48 *alt.* Ps. *59*; 60 (67) Deut. 10. 12–end Eph. 5. 1–14	**W**		Exod. ch. 33 Luke 3. 15–22	Deut. 10. 12–end Eph. 5. 1–14
Ps. 81; *85* *alt.* Ps. 61; *62*; 64 Deut. 11. 8–end Eph. 5. 15–end	**W**		Exod. 34. 1–10, 27–end Luke 4. 1–13	Deut. 11. 8–end Eph. 5. 15–end
Ps. *36*; 40 *alt.* Ps. 38 Deut. 12. 1–14 Eph. 6. 1–9	**W**		Exod. 35.20 – 36.7 Luke 4. 14–30	Deut. 12. 1–14 Eph. 6. 1–9
Ps. *84*; 86 *alt.* Ps. 65; *66* Deut. 15. 1–18 Eph. 6. 10–end ct	**W**		Exod. 40. 17–end Luke 4. 31–37	Deut. 15. 1–18 Eph. 6. 10–end ct

May 2006

| | Sunday Principal Service / Weekday Eucharist | Third Service / Morning Prayer |

14 S   THE FIFTH SUNDAY OF EASTER
(Matthias transferred to 15th)

| *The reading from Acts must be used as either the first or second reading at the Principal Service* | Acts 8. 26–end [Baruch 3.9–15, 32 – 4.4 *or* Gen. 22. 1–18] Ps. 22. 25–end 1 John 4. 7–end John 15. 1–8 | Ps. 44. 16–end 2 Macc. 7. 7–14 *or* Dan. 3. 16–28 Heb. 11.32 – 12.2 |

W

15 M   MATTHIAS THE APOSTLE (transferred from 14th)*

| *The reading from Acts must be used as either the first or second reading at the Eucharist.* | Isa. 22. 15–end *or* Acts 1. 15–end Ps. 15 Acts 1. 15–end *or* 1 Cor. 4. 1–7 John 15. 9–17 | *MP:* Ps. 16; 147. 1–12 1 Sam. 2. 27–35 Acts 2. 37–end |

or, if Matthias is celebrated on 24 February:

| | Acts 14. 5–18 Ps. 118. 1–3, 14–15 John 14. 21–26 | Ps. 145 *alt.* Ps. 71 Num. 9. 15–end; 10. 33–end |

R   Luke 4. 38–end

16 Tu   *Caroline Chisholm, Social Reformer, 1877*

| | Acts 14. 19–end Ps. 145. 10–end John 14. 27–end | Ps. *19*; 147. 1–12 *alt.* Ps. 73 Num. 11. 1–33 |

W   Luke 5. 1–11

17 W

| | Acts 15. 1–6 Ps. 122. 1–5 John 15. 1–8 | Ps. *30*; 147. 13–end *alt.* Ps. 77 Num. ch. 12 |

W   Luke 5. 12–26

18 Th

| | Acts 15. 7–21 Ps. 96. 1–3, 7–10 John 15. 9–11 | Ps. *57*; 148 *alt.* Ps. 78. 1–39† Num. 13. 1–3, 17–end |

W   Luke 5. 27–end

19 F   **Dunstan, Archbishop of Canterbury, Restorer of Monastic Life, 988**

| Com. Bishop *esp.* Matt. 24. 42–46 *also* Exod. 31. 1–5 | *or* Acts 15. 22–31 Ps. 57. 8–end John 15. 12–17 | Ps. *138*; 149 *alt.* Ps. 55 Num. 14. 1–25 |

W   Luke 6. 1–11

20 Sa   **Alcuin of York, Deacon, Abbot of Tours, 804**

| Com. Religious *also* Col. 3. 12–16 John 4. 19–24 | *or* Acts 16. 1–10 Ps. 100 John 15. 18–21 | Ps. *146*; 150 *alt.* Ps. *76*; 79 Num. 14. 26–end |

W   Luke 6. 12–26

21 S   THE SIXTH SUNDAY OF EASTER

| *The reading from Acts must be used as either the first or second reading at the Principal Service* | Acts 10. 44–end [Isa. 55. 1–11] Ps. 98 1 John 5. 1–6 John 15. 9–17 | Ps. 104. 26–32 Ezek. 47. 1–12 John 21. 1–19 |

W

22 M   Rogation Day**

| | Acts 16. 11–15 Ps. 149. 1–5 John 15.26 – 16.4 | Ps. *65*; 67 *alt.* Ps. *80*; 82 Num. 16. 1–35 |

W   Luke 6. 27–38

*Matthias may be celebrated on 24 February instead of 14 May.
**For Rogation Day provision, see p. 12.

Second Service Evening Prayer	Calendar and Holy Communion	Morning Prayer	Evening Prayer
	THE FOURTH SUNDAY AFTER EASTER		
Ps. 96	Job 19. 21–27a	Ps. 44. 15–end	Ps. 96
Isa. 60. 1–14	Ps. 66. 14–end	2 Macc. 7. 7–14	Isa. 60. 1–14
Rev. 3. 1–13	James 1. 17–21	*or* Dan. 3. 16–28	Rev. 3. 1–13
Gospel: Mark 16. 9–16	John 16. 5–15	Heb. 11.32 – 12.2	
or First EP of Matthias			
Ps. 147			
Isa. 22. 15–22			
Phil. 3.13b – 4.1			
R ct	W		
EP: Ps. 80		Num. 9. 15–end;	Deut. 16. 1–20
1 Sam. 16. 1–13a		10. 33–end	1 Pet. 1. 1–12
Matt. 7. 15–27		Luke 4. 38–end	
Ps. 105			
alt. Ps. *72*; 75			
Deut. 16. 1–20			
1 Pet. 1. 1–12	W		
Ps. 96; *97*		Num. 11. 1–33	Deut. 17. 8–end
alt. Ps. 74		Luke 5. 1–11	1 Pet. 1. 13–end
Deut. 17. 8–end			
1 Pet. 1. 13–end	W		
Ps. 98; *99*; 100		Num. ch. 12	Deut. 18. 9–end
alt. Ps. 119. 81–104		Luke 5. 12–26	1 Pet. 2. 1–10
Deut. 18. 9–end			
1 Pet. 2. 1–10	W		
Ps. 104		Num. 13. 1–3,	Deut. ch. 19
alt. Ps. 78. 40–end†		17–end	1 Pet. 2. 11–end
Deut. ch. 19		Luke 5. 27–end	
1 Pet. 2. 11–end	W		
	Dunstan, Archbishop of Canterbury, Restorer of Monastic Life, 988		
Ps. 66	Com. Bishop	Num. 14. 1–25	Deut. 21.22 – 22.8
alt. Ps. 69		Luke 6. 1–11	1 Pet. 3. 1–12
Deut. 21.22 – 22.8			
1 Pet. 3. 1–12	W		
Ps. 118		Num. 14. 26–end	Deut. 24. 5–end
alt. Ps. 81; *84*		Luke 6. 12–26	1 Pet. 3. 13–end
Deut. 24. 5–end			
1 Pet. 3. 13–end			
ct	W		ct
	THE FIFTH SUNDAY AFTER EASTER		
	Rogation Sunday		
Ps. 45	Joel 2. 21–26	Ps. 104. 26–32	Ps. 45
Song of Sol. 4.16 – 5.2;	Ps. 66. 1–8	Ezek. 47. 1–12	Song of Sol.
8. 6–7	James 1. 22–end	John 21. 1–19	4.16 – 5.2; 8. 6–7
Rev. 3. 14–end	John 16. 23b–end		Rev. 3. 14–end
Gospel: Luke 22. 24–30	W		
	Rogation Day		
Ps. *121*; 122; 123	Job 28. 1–11	Num. 16. 1–35	Deut. ch. 26
alt. Ps. *85*; 86	Ps. 107. 1–9	Luke 6. 27–38	1 Pet. 4. 1–11
Deut. ch. 26	James 5. 7–11		
1 Pet. 4. 1–11	W Luke 6. 36–42		

May 2006

	Sunday Principal Service Weekday Eucharist	Third Service Morning Prayer

23 Tu Rogation Day*

Acts 16. 22–34
Ps. 138
John 16. 5–11

Ps. 124; 125; *126*; 127
alt. Ps. 87; *89. 1–18*
Num. 16. 36–end

W

Luke 6. 39–end

---

24 W **John and Charles Wesley, Evangelists, Hymn Writers, 1791 and 1788**
Rogation Day*
Com. Pastor   *or* Acts 17.15, 22 – 18.1
also Eph. 5. 15–20   Ps. 148. 1–2, 11–end
                              John 16. 12–15

Ps. *132*; 133
alt. Ps. 119. 105–128
Num. 17. 1–11

W

Luke 7. 1–10

---

25 Th **ASCENSION DAY**
The reading from Acts must   Acts 1. 1–11
be used as either the first or   *or* Dan. 7. 9–14
second reading at the   Ps. 47 *or* Ps. 93
Eucharist.   Eph. 1. 15–end
                                or Acts 1. 1–11

MP: Ps. 110
Isa. 52. 7–end
Heb. 7. [11–25]26–end

Ⓦ   Luke 24. 44–end

---

26 F **Augustine, first Archbishop of Canterbury, 605**
John Calvin, Reformer, 1564; Philip Neri, Founder of the Oratorians, Spiritual Guide, 1595
Com. Bishop   *or* Acts 18. 9–18
also 1 Thess. 2. 2b–8   Ps. 47. 1–6
Matt. 13. 31–33   John 16. 20–23

Ps. 20; *81*
alt. Ps. *88*; (95)
Num. 20. 1–13
Luke 7. 11–17
[Exod. 35.30 – 36.1

W

Gal. 5. 13–end]**

---

27 Sa

Acts 18. 22–end
Ps. 47. 1–2, 7–end
John 16. 23–28

Ps. 21; *47*
alt. Ps. 96; *97*; 100
Num. 21. 4–9
Luke 7. 18–35
[Num. 11. 16–17, 24–29

W

1 Cor. ch. 2]

---

28 S THE SEVENTH SUNDAY OF EASTER (SUNDAY AFTER ASCENSION DAY)
The reading from Acts must   Acts 1. 15–17, 21–end
be used as either the first or   [Ezek. 36. 24–28]
second reading at the   Ps. 1
Principal Service   1 John 5. 9–13

Ps. 76
Isa. 14. 3–15
Rev. 14. 1–13

W

John 17. 6–19

---

29 M

Acts 19. 1–8
Ps. 68. 1–6
John 16. 29–end

Ps. *93*; 96; 97
alt. Ps. *98*; 99; 101
Num. 22. 1–35
Luke 7. 36–end
[Num. 27. 15–end

W

1 Cor. ch. 3]

---

30 Tu **Josephine Butler, Social Reformer, 1906**
Joan of Arc, Visionary, 1431; Apolo Kivebulaya, Evangelist in Central Africa, 1933
Com. Saint   *or* Acts 20. 17–27
esp. Isa. 58. 6–11   Ps. 68. 9–10, 18–19
also 1 John 3. 18–23   John 17. 1–11
Matt. 9. 10–13

Ps. 98; *99*; 100
alt. Ps. *106*† (or 103)
Num. 22.36 – 23.12
Luke 8. 1–15
[1 Sam. 10. 1–10
1 Cor. 12. 1–13]

W

---

*For Rogation Day provision, see p. 12.
**The alternative readings in square brackets may be used at one of the offices, in preparation for the Day of Pentecost.

Second Service Evening Prayer	Calendar and Holy Communion	Morning Prayer	Evening Prayer
Ps. *128*; 129; 130; 131 *alt.* Ps. 89. 19–end Deut. 28. 1–14 1 Pet. 4. 12–end	Rogation Day Deut. 8. 1–10 Ps. 121 James 5. 16–end **W** Luke 11. 5–13	Num. 16. 36–end Luke 6. 39–end	Deut. 28. 1–14 1 Pet. 4. 12–end
First EP of Ascension Day Ps. 15; 24 2 Sam. 23. 1–5 Col. 2.20 – 3.4 𝖂 ct	Rogation Day Deut. 34. 1–7 Ps. 108. 1–6 Eph. 4. 7–13 **W** John 17. 1–11	Num. 17. 1–11 Luke 7. 1–10	*First EP of Ascension Day* Ps. 15; 24 2 Sam. 23. 1–5 Col. 2.20 – 3.4 𝖂 ct
EP: Ps. 8 Song of the Three 29–37 *or* 2 Kings 2. 1–15 Rev. ch. 5 *Gospel:* Matt. 28. 16–end	**ASCENSION DAY** Dan. 7. 13–14 Ps. 68. 1–6 Acts 1. 1–11 Mark 16. 14–20 *or* Luke 24. 44–end 𝖂	Ps. 110 Isa. 52. 7–end Heb. 7. [11–25]26–end	Ps. 8 Song of the Three 29–37 *or* 2 Kings 2. 1–15 Rev. ch. 5
Ps. 145 *alt.* Ps. 102 Deut. 29. 2–15 1 John 1.1 – 2.6	**Augustine, first Archbishop of Canterbury, 605** Com. Bishop *or* Ascension CEG **W**	Num. 20. 1–13 Luke 7. 11–17 [Exod. 35.30 – 36.1 Gal. 5. 13–end]**	Deut. 29. 2–15 1 John 1.1 – 2.6
Ps. 84; *85* *alt.* Ps. 104 Deut. ch. 30 1 John 2. 7–17 ct	Ascension CEG **W**	Num. 21. 4–9 Luke 7. 18–35 [Num. 11. 16–17, 24–29 1 Cor. ch. 2]	Deut. ch. 30 1 John 2. 7–17 ct
Ps. 147. 1–12 Isa. ch. 61 Luke 4. 14–21	THE SUNDAY AFTER ASCENSION DAY 2 Kings 2. 9–15 Ps. 68. 32–end 1 Pet. 4. 7–11 John 15.26 – 16.4a **W**	Ps. 76 Isa. 14. 3–15 Rev. 14. 1–13	Ps. 147. 1–12 Isa. ch. 61 Luke 4. 14–21
Ps. 18 *alt.* Ps. *105*† (*or* 103) Deut. 31. 1–13 1 John 2. 18–end **W**		Num. 22. 1–35 Luke 7. 36–end [Num. 27. 15–end 1 Cor. ch. 3]	Deut. 31. 1–13 1 John 2. 18–end
Ps. 68 *alt.* Ps. 107† Deut. 31. 14–29 1 John 3. 1–10 *or First EP of The Visit of* *Mary to Elizabeth* Ps. 45 Song of Sol. 2. 8–14 Luke 1. 26–38 ct	 **W**	Num. 22.36 – 23.12 Luke 8. 1–15 [1 Sam. 10. 1–10 1 Cor. 12. 1–13]	Deut. 31. 14–29 1 John 3. 1–10

May 2006

		Sunday Principal Service Weekday Eucharist	Third Service Morning Prayer
31	W	THE VISIT OF THE BLESSED VIRGIN MARY TO ELIZABETH* Zeph. 3. 14–18 Ps. 113 Rom. 12. 9–16	*MP*: Ps. 85; 150 1 Sam. 2. 1–10 Mark 3. 31–end
	W	Luke 1. 39–49 [50–56]	
		or, if The Visitation is *celebrated on 2, 3 or 4 July:* Acts 20. 28–end Ps. 68. 27–28, 32–end John 17. 11–19	Ps. 2; *29* *alt.* Ps. 110; *111*; 112 Num. 23. 13–end Luke 8. 16–25 [1 Kings 19. 1–18 Matt. 3. 13–end]
	W		

June 2006

1	Th	**Justin, Martyr at Rome, *c*. 165** Com. Martyr *or* *esp.* John 15. 18–21 *also* 1 Macc. 2. 15–22 1 Cor. 1. 18–25	Acts 22. 30; 23. 6–11 Ps. 16. 1, 5–end John 17. 20–end	Ps. *24*; 72 *alt.* Ps. 113; *115* Num. ch. 24 Luke 8. 26–39 [Ezek. 11. 14–20
	Wr			Matt. 9.35 – 10.20]
2	F		Acts 25. 13–21 Ps. 103. 1–2, 11–12, 19–20 John 21. 15–19	Ps. *28*; 30 *alt.* Ps. 139 Num. 27. 12–end Luke 8. 40–end [Ezek. 36. 22–28
	W			Matt. 12. 22–32]
3	Sa	*The Martyrs of Uganda, 1885–7 and 1977*	Acts 28. 16–20, 30–end Ps. 11. 4–end John 21. 20–25	Ps. 42; *43* *alt.* Ps. 120; *121*; 122 Num. 32. 1–27 Luke 9. 1–17 [Mic. 3. 1–8
	W			Eph. 6. 10–20]
4	S	**DAY OF PENTECOST (Whit Sunday)** *The reading from Acts* *must be used as either the* *first or second reading at* *the Principal Service*	Acts 2. 1–21 *or* Ezek. 37. 1–14 Ps. 104. 26–36, 37b (*or* 26–end) Rom. 8. 22–27 *or* Acts 2. 1–21	*MP*: Ps. 145 Isa. 11. 1–9 *or* Wisd. 7. 15–23 [24–27] 1 Cor. 12. 4–13
	R		John 15. 26–27; 16. 4b–15	
5 DEL 9	M	**Boniface (Wynfrith) of Crediton, Bishop, Apostle of Germany, Martyr, 754** Ordinary Time resumes today Com. Martyr *or* *also* Acts 20. 24–28	2 Pet. 1. 2–7 Ps. 91. 1–2, 14–end	Ps. 123; 124; 125; *126* Josh. ch. 1
	Gr		Mark 12. 1–12	Luke 9. 18–27
6	Tu	*Ini Kopuria, Founder of the Melanesian Brotherhood, 1945*	2 Pet. 3. 11–15a, 17–end Ps. 90. 1–4, 10, 14, 16	Ps. *132*; 133 Josh. ch. 2
	G		Mark 12. 13–17	Luke 9. 28–36
7	W		2 Tim. 1. 1–3, 6–12 Ps. 123	Ps. 119. 153–end Josh. ch. 3
	G		Mark 12. 18–27	Luke 9. 37–50
8	Th	**Thomas Ken, Bishop of Bath and Wells, Nonjuror, Hymn Writer, 1711** Com. Bishop *or* *esp.* 2 Cor. 4. 1–10	2 Tim. 2. 8–15 Ps. 25. 4–12	Ps. *143*; 146 Josh. 4.1 – 5.1
	Gw	Matt. 24. 42–46	Mark 12. 28–34	Luke 9. 51–end

*The Visit of the Blessed Virgin Mary to Elizabeth may be celebrated on 2 July or transferred to 4 July or, if Thomas the Apostle is celebrated on 21 December, transferred to 3 July.

Second Service Evening Prayer	Calendar and Holy Communion	Morning Prayer	Evening Prayer
EP: Ps. 122; 127; 128 Zech. 2. 10–end John 3. 25–30		Num. 23. 13–end Luke 8. 16–25 [1 Kings 18. 1–18 Matt. 3. 13–end]	Deut. 31.30 – 32.14 1 John 3. 11–end
Ps. 36; *46* *alt.* Ps. 119. 129–152 Deut. 31.30 – 32.14 1 John 3. 11–end	W		
Ps. 139 *alt.* Ps. 114; *116*; 117 Deut. 32. 15–47 1 John 4. 1–6	**Nicomede, Priest and Martyr at Rome (date unknown)** Com. Martyr	Num. ch. 24 Luke 8. 26–39 [Ezek. 11. 14–20 Matt. 9.35 – 10.20]	Deut. 32. 15–47 1 John 4. 1–6
Ps. 147 *alt.* Ps. *130*; 131; 137 Deut. ch. 33 1 John 4. 7–end	Wr	Num. 27. 12–end Luke 8. 40–end [Ezek. 36. 22–28 Matt. 12. 22–32]	Deut. ch. 33 1 John 4. 7–end
First EP of Pentecost Ps. 48 Deut. 16. 9–15 John 7. 37–39	W	Num. 32. 1–27 Luke 9. 1–17 [Mic. 3. 1–8 Eph. 6. 10–20]	*First EP of Whit Sunday* Ps. 48 Deut. 16. 9–15 John 7. 37–39
R ct	W		R ct
EP: Ps. 139. 1–11 [13–18, 23–24] Ezek. 36. 22–28 Acts 2. 22–38 *Gospel*: John 20. 19–23	**WHIT SUNDAY** Deut. 16. 9–12 Ps. 122 Acts 2. 1–11 John 14. 15–31a R	Ps. 145 Isa. 11. 1–9 *or* Wisd. 7. 15–23 [24–27] 1 Cor. 12. 4–13	Ps. 139. 1–11 [13–18, 23–24] Ezek. 36. 22–28 Acts 2. 22–38
Ps. *127*; 128; 129 2 Chron. 17. 1–12 Rom. 1. 1–17	**Monday in Whitsun Week** Acts 10. 34–end John 3. 16–21 R	Ezek. 11. 14–20 Acts 2. 12–36	Exod. 35.30 – 36.1 Acts 2. 37–end
Ps. (134) *135* 2 Chron. 18. 1–27 Rom. 1. 18–end	**Tuesday in Whitsun Week** Acts 8. 14–17 John 10. 1–10 R	Ezek. 37. 1–14 1 Cor. 12. 1–13	2 Sam. 23. 1–5 1 Cor. 12.27 – 13.end
Ps. 136 2 Chron. 18.28 – 19.end Rom. 2. 1–16	**Ember Day** Ember CEG *or* Acts 2. 14–21 John 6. 44–51 R	Josh. ch. 3 Luke 9. 37–50	2 Chron. 18.28 – 19.end Rom. 2. 1–16
Ps. *138*; 140; 141 2 Chron. 20. 1–23 Rom. 2. 17–end	Acts 2. 22–28 Luke 9. 1–6 R	Josh. 4.1 – 5.1 Luke 9. 51–end	2 Chron. 20. 1–23 Rom. 2. 17–end

June 2006

		Sunday Principal Service Weekday Eucharist		Third Service Morning Prayer

9 **F** **Columba, Abbot of Iona, Missionary, 597**
Ephrem of Syria, Deacon, Hymn Writer, Teacher, 373

	Com. Missionary	*or*	2 Tim. 3. 10–end	Ps. *142*; 144
	also Titus 2. 11–15		Ps. 119. 161–168	Josh. 5. 2–end
Gw			Mark 12. 35–37	Luke 10. 1–16

10 **Sa**

2 Tim. 4. 1–8	Ps. 147
Ps. 71. 7–16	Josh. 6. 1–20
Mark 12. 38–end	Luke 10. 17–24

G

---

11 **S** **TRINITY SUNDAY**
(Barnabas transferred to 12th)

Isa. 6. 1–8	*MP*: Ps. 33. 1–12
Ps. 29	Prov. 8. 1–4, 22–31
Rom. 8. 12–17	2 Cor. 13. [5–10] 11–end
John 3. 1–17	

℣

---

12 **M** **BARNABAS THE APOSTLE (transferred from 11th)**

DEL 10

The reading from Acts	Job 29. 11–16	*MP*: Ps. 100; 101; 117
must be used as either the	*or* Acts 11. 19–30	Jer. 9. 23–24
first or second reading at	Ps. 112	Acts 4. 32–end
the Eucharist.	Acts 11. 19–end	
	or Gal. 2. 1–10	
R	John 15. 12–17	

13 **Tu**

1 Kings. 17. 7–16	Ps. *5*; 6 (8)
Ps. 4	Josh. 7. 16–end
G Matt. 5. 13–16	Luke 10. 38–end

14 **W** *Richard Baxter, Puritan Divine, 1691*

1 Kings 18. 20–39	Ps. 119. 1–32
Ps. 16. 1, 6–end	Josh. 8. 1–29
Matt. 5. 17–19	Luke 11. 1–13

G

---

15 **Th** **DAY OF THANKSGIVING FOR HOLY COMMUNION (CORPUS CHRISTI)**
Evelyn Underhill, Spiritual Writer, 1941

Gen. 14. 18–20	*MP*: Ps. 147
Ps. 116. 10–end	Deut. 8. 2–16
1 Cor. 11. 23–26	1 Cor. 10. 1–17
W John 6. 51–58	

or the Ferial readings for	1 Kings 18. 41–end	Ps. 14; *15*; 16
the day:	Ps. 65. 8–end	Josh. 8. 30–end
G	Matt. 5. 20–26	Luke 11. 14–28

16 **F** **Richard, Bishop of Chichester, 1253**
Joseph Butler, Bishop of Durham, Philosopher, 1752

	Com. Bishop	*or*	1 Kings 19. 9, 11–16	Ps. 17; *19*
	also John 21. 15–19		Ps. 27. 8–16	Josh. 9. 3–26
Gw			Matt. 5. 27–32	Luke 11. 29–36

Second Service Evening Prayer	Calendar and Holy Communion		Morning Prayer	Evening Prayer
Ps. 145 2 Chron. 22.10 – 23.end Rom. 3. 1–20	Ember Day Ember CEG or Acts 8. 5–8 Luke 5. 17–26	R	Josh. 5. 2–end Luke 10. 1–16	2 Chron. 22.10 – 23.end Rom. 3. 1–20
First EP of Trinity Sunday Ps. 97; 98 Isa. 40. 12–31 Mark 1. 1–13 ℬ ct	Ember Day Ember CEG or Acts 13. 44–end Matt. 20. 29–end	R	Josh. 6. 1–20 Luke 10. 17–24	First EP of Trinity Sunday Ps. 97; 98 Isa. 40. 12–end Mark 1. 1–13 ℬ ct
EP: Ps. 104. 1–10 Ezek. 1. 4–10, 22–28a Rev. ch. 4 Gospel: Mark 1. 1–13 or First EP of Barnabas Ps. 1; 15 Isa. 42. 5–12 Acts 14. 8–end R ct	**TRINITY SUNDAY** (Barnabas transferred to 12th) Isa. 6. 1–8 Ps. 8 Rev. 4. 1–11 John 3. 1–15	ℬ	Ps. 33. 1–12 Prov. 8. 1–4, 22–31 2 Cor. 13. [5–10] 11–end	Ps. 104. 1–10 Ezek. 1. 4–10, 22–28a Mark 1. 1–13 or First EP of Barnabas (Ps. 1; 15) Isa. 42. 5–12 Acts 14. 8–end R ct
EP: Ps. 147 Eccles. 12. 9–end or Tobit 4. 5–11 Acts 9. 26–31	**BARNABAS THE APOSTLE (transferred from 11th)** Ps. 112 Job 29. 11–16 Acts 11. 22–end John 15. 12–16	R	(Ps. 100; 101; 117) Jer. 9. 23–24 Acts 4. 32–end	(Ps. 147) Eccles. 12. 9–end or Tobit 4. 5–11 Acts 9. 26–31
Ps. 9; 10† 2 Chron. ch. 28 Rom. 4. 13–end		G	Josh. 7. 16–end Luke 10. 38–end	2 Chron. ch. 28 Rom. 4. 13–end
Ps. 11; 12; 13 2 Chron. 29. 1–19 Rom. 5. 1–11 or First EP of Corpus Christi Ps. 110; 111 Exod. 16. 2–15 John 6. 22–35 W ct		G	Josh. 8. 1–29 Luke 11. 1–13	2 Chron. 29. 1–19 Rom. 5. 1–11
	To celebrate Corpus Christi, see Common Worship provision.			
EP: Ps. 23; 42; 43 Prov. 9. 1–5 Luke 9. 11–17			Josh. 8. 30–end Luke 11. 14–28	2 Chron. 29. 20–end Rom. 5. 12–end
Ps. 18† 2 Chron. 29. 20–end Rom. 5. 12–end		G		
Ps. 22 2 Chron. ch. 30 Rom. 6. 1–14		G	Josh. 9. 3–26 Luke 11. 29–36	2 Chron. ch. 30 Rom. 6. 1–14

June 2006

	Sunday Principal Service / Weekday Eucharist	Third Service / Morning Prayer

17 Sa

Samuel and Henrietta Barnett, Social Reformers, 1913 and 1936
1 Kings 19. 19–end   Ps. 20; 21; *23*
Ps. 16. 1–7   Josh. 10. 1–15
Matt. 5. 33–37   Luke 11. 37–end

G

18 S

THE FIRST SUNDAY AFTER TRINITY (Proper 6)
Track 1   Track 2   Ps. 42; 43
1 Sam. 15.34 – 16.13   Ezek. 17. 22–end   Deut. 10.12 – 11.1
Ps. 20   Ps. 92. 1–4, 12–end (*or* 1–8) Acts 23. 12–35
2 Cor. 5. 6–10 [11–13] 14–17   2 Cor. 5. 6–10 [11–13] 14–17
Mark 4. 26–34   Mark 4. 26–34

G

19 M
DEL 11

Sundar Singh of India, Sadhu (holy man), Evangelist, Teacher, 1929
1 Kings 21. 1–16   Ps. 27; *30*
Ps. 5. 1–5   Josh. ch. 14
Matt. 5. 38–42   Luke 12. 1–12

G

20 Tu

1 Kings 21. 17–end   Ps. 32; *36*
Ps. 51. 1–9   Josh. 21.43 – 22.8
Matt. 5. 43–end   Luke 12. 13–21

G

21 W

2 Kings 2. 1, 6–14   Ps. 34
Ps. 31. 21–end   Josh. 22. 9–end
Matt. 6. 1–6, 16–18   Luke 12. 22–31

G *or* R

22 Th

Alban, first Martyr of Britain, c. 250
Com. Martyr   *or* Ecclus. 48. 1–14   Ps. 37†
esp. 2 Tim. 2. 3–13   *or* Isa. 63. 7–9   Josh. ch. 23
John 12. 24–26   Ps. 97. 1–8   Luke 12. 32–40
                         Matt. 6. 7–15

Gr

23 F

Etheldreda, Abbess of Ely, c. 678
Com. Religious   *or* 2 Kings 11. 1–4, 9–18, 20   Ps. 31
also Matt. 25. 1–13   Ps. 132. 1–5, 11–13   Josh. 24. 1–28
                         Matt. 6. 19–23   Luke 12. 41–48

Gw *or* Rw

24 Sa

THE BIRTH OF JOHN THE BAPTIST
Isa. 40. 1–11   *MP*: Ps. 50; 149
Ps. 85. 7–end   Ecclus. 48. 1–10
Acts 13. 14b–26   *or* Mal. 3. 1–6
or Gal. 3. 23–end   Luke 3. 1–17

W
Luke 1. 57–66, 80

25 S

THE SECOND SUNDAY AFTER TRINITY (Proper 7)
Track 1   Track 2
1 Sam. 17. [1a, 4–11, 19–23]   Job 38. 1–11   Ps. 48
32–49   Ps. 107. [1–3] 23–32   Deut. 11. 1–15
and Ps. 9. 9–end   2 Cor. 6. 1–13   Acts 27. 1–12
or 1 Sam. 17.57 – 18.5, 10–16   Mark 4. 35–end
and Ps. 133
2 Cor. 6. 1–13
Mark 4. 35–end

G

26 M
DEL 12

2 Kings 17. 5–8, 13–15, 18   Ps. 44
Ps. 60. 1–5, 11–end   Judg. ch. 2
Matt. 7. 1–5   Luke 13. 1–9

G

27 T

Cyril, Bishop of Alexandria, Teacher, 444
2 Kings 19. 9–11, 14–21a, 31–36   Ps. *48*; 52
Ps. 48. 1–2, 8–end   Judg. 4. 1–23
Matt. 7. 6, 12–14   Luke 13. 10–21

G

Second Service Evening Prayer	Calendar and Holy Communion	Morning Prayer	Evening Prayer
	Alban, first Martyr of Britain, *c.* 250		
Ps. *24*; 25	Com. Martyr	Josh. 10. 1–15	2 Chron. 32. 1–22
2 Chron. 32. 1–22		Luke 11. 37–end	Rom. 6. 15–end
Rom. 6. 15–end			
ct	Gr		ct
	THE FIRST SUNDAY AFTER TRINITY		
Ps. 39	2 Sam. 9. 6–end	Ps. 42; 43	Ps. 39
Jer. 7. 1–16	Ps. 41. 1–4	Deut. 10.12 – 11.1	Jer. 7. 1–16
Rom. 9. 14–26	1 John 4. 7–end	Acts 23. 12–35	Rom. 9. 14–26
Gospel: Luke 7.36 – 8.3	Luke 16. 19–31		
	G		
		Josh. ch. 14	2 Chron. 33. 1–13
Ps. 26; *28*; 29		Luke 12. 1–12	Rom. 7. 1–6
2 Chron. 33. 1–13			
Rom. 7. 1–6	G		
	Translation of Edward, King of the West Saxons, 979		
Ps. 33	Com. Martyr	Josh. 21.43 – 22.8	2 Chron. 34. 1–18
2 Chron. 34. 1–18		Luke 12. 13–21	Rom. 7. 7–end
Rom. 7. 7–end	Gr		
Ps. 119. 33–56		Josh. 22. 9–end	2 Chron. 34. 19–end
2 Chron. 34. 19–end		Luke 12. 22–31	Rom. 8. 1–11
Rom. 8. 1–11	G		
Ps. 39; *40*		Josh. ch. 23	2 Chron. 35. 1–19
2 Chron. 35. 1–19		Luke 12. 32–40	Rom. 8. 12–17
Rom. 8. 12–17			
	G		
Ps. 35		Josh. 24. 1–28	2 Chron. 35.20 – 36.10
2 Chron. 35.20 – 36.10		Luke 12. 41–48	Rom. 8. 18–30
Rom. 8. 18–30			*or First EP of The*
or First EP of The Birth of			*Nativity of John the*
John the Baptist			*Baptist*
Ps. 71			(Ps. 71)
Judges 13. 2–7, 24–25			Judges 13. 2–7, 24–25
Luke 1. 5–25			Luke 1. 5–25
W ct	G		**W ct**
	THE NATIVITY OF JOHN THE BAPTIST		
EP: Ps. 80; 82	Isa. 40. 1–11	(Ps. 50; 149)	(Ps. 82)
Mal. ch. 4	Ps. 80. 1–7	Ecclus. 48. 1–10	Mal. ch. 4
Matt. 11. 2–19	Acts 13. 22–26	*or* Mal. 3. 1–6	Matt. 11. 2–19
	Luke 1. 57–80	Luke 3. 1–17	
	W		
	THE SECOND SUNDAY AFTER TRINITY		
Ps. 49	Gen. 12. 1–4	Ps. 48	Ps. 49
Jer. 10. 1–16	Ps. 120	Deut. 11. 1–15	Jer. 10. 1–16
Rom. 11. 25–36	1 John 3. 13–end	Acts 27. 1–12	Rom. 11. 25–36
Gospel: Luke 8. 26–39	Luke 14. 16–24		
	G		
Ps. *47*; 49		Judg. ch. 2	Ezra ch. 1
Ezra ch. 1		Luke 13. 1–9	Rom. 9. 1–18
Rom. 9. 1–18	G		
Ps. 50		Judg. 4. 1–23	Ezra ch. 3
Ezra ch. 3		Luke 13. 10–21	Rom. 9. 19–end
Rom. 9. 19–end	G		

June 2006

		Sunday Principal Service Weekday Eucharist		Third Service Morning Prayer

28 W

Irenaeus, Bishop of Lyons, Teacher, c. 200
Ember Day*
Com. Teacher   or 2 Kings 22. 8–13; 23. 1–3   Ps. 119. 57–80
also 2 Pet. 1. 16–21   Ps. 119. 33–40   Judg. ch. 5
                         Matt. 7. 15–end   Luke 13. 22–end

Gw or Rw

29 Th

PETER AND PAUL, APOSTLES
The reading from Acts   Zech. 4. 1–6a, 10b–end   MP: Ps. 71; 113
must be used as either the   or Acts 12. 1–11   Isa. 49. 1–6
first or second reading at   Ps. 125   Acts 11. 1–18
the Eucharist.   Acts 12. 1–11
R   or 2 Tim. 4. 6–8, 17–18
                             Matt. 16. 13–19

or, if Peter is commemorated alone:
The reading from Acts must   Ezek. 3. 22–end   MP: Ps. 71; 113
be used as either the first or or Acts 12. 1–11   Isa. 49. 1–6
second reading at the   Ps. 125   Acts 11. 1–18
Eucharist.   Acts 12. 1–11
R   or 2 Tim. 4. 6–8, 17–18
                             Matt. 16. 13–19

30 F

Ember Day*
                             2 Kings 25. 1–12   Ps. 51; 54
                             Ps. 137. 1–6   Judg. 6. 25–end
G or R   Matt. 8. 1–4   Luke 14. 12–24

July 2006

1 Sa

Ember Day*
Henry, John and Henry Venn the Younger, Priests, Evangelical Divines, 1797, 1813 and 1873
                             Lam. 2. 2, 10–14, 18–19   Ps. 68
                             Ps. 74. 1–3, 21–end   Judg. ch. 7
                             Matt. 8. 5–17   Luke 14. 25–end
G or R

2 S

THE THIRD SUNDAY AFTER TRINITY (Proper 8)**
Track 1   Track 2
2 Sam. 1. 1, 17–end   Wisd. of Sol. 1. 13–15; 2. 23–24 Ps. 56
Ps. 130   Canticle: Lam. 3. 23–33   Deut. 15. 1–11
2 Cor. 8. 7–end   or Ps. 30   Acts 27. [13–32] 33–end
Mark 5. 21–end   2 Cor. 8. 7–end
                             Mark 5. 21–end

G

3 M

THOMAS THE APOSTLE***
                             Hab. 2. 1–4   MP: Ps. 92; 146
DEL 13   Ps. 31. 1–6   2 Sam. 15. 17–21
                             Eph. 2. 19–end   or Ecclus. ch. 2
                             John 20. 24–29   John 11. 1–16
R   Amos 2. 6–10, 13–end   Ps. 71
or, if Thomas is not   Ps. 50. 16–23   Judg. 8. 22–end
celebrated:
G   Matt. 8. 18–22   Luke 15. 1–10

4 Tu

                             Amos 3. 1–8; 4. 11–12   Ps. 73
                             Ps. 5. 8–end   Judg. 9. 1–21
G   Matt. 8. 23–27   Luke 15. 11–end

---

*For Ember Day provision, see p. 13.
**The Visitation of the Blessed Virgin Mary to Elizabeth may be celebrated on 2 July or transferred to 3 July (if Thomas the Apostle
is celebrated on 21 December) or 4 July instead of 31 May.
***Thomas the Apostle may be celebrated on 21 December instead of 3 July.

Second Service Evening Prayer	Calendar and Holy Communion	Morning Prayer	Evening Prayer
Ps. *59*; 60 (67) Ezra 4. 1–5 Rom. 10. 1–10 *or First EP of Peter and Paul* Ps. 66; 67 Ezek. 3. 4–11 Gal. 1.13 – 2.8 *or, for Peter alone:* Acts 9. 32–end **R** ct	G	Judg. ch. 5 Luke 13. 22–end	Ezra 4. 1–5 Rom. 10. 1–10 *or First EP of Peter* (Ps. 66; 67) Ezek. 3. 4–11 Acts 9. 32–end **R** ct
EP: Ps. 124; 138 Ezek. 34. 11–16 John 21. 15–22	**PETER THE APOSTLE** Ezek. 3. 4–11 Ps. 125 Acts 12. 1–11 Matt. 16. 13–19	(Ps. 71; 113) Isa. 49. 1–6 Acts 11. 1–18	(Ps. 124; 138) Ezek. 34. 11–16 John 21. 15–22
EP: Ps. 124; 138 Ezek. 34. 11–16 John 21. 15–22	R		
Ps. 38 Ezra ch. 5 Rom. 11. 1–12	G	Judg. 6. 25–end Luke 14. 12–24	Ezra ch. 5 Rom. 11. 1–12
Ps. 65; *66* Ezra ch. 6 Rom. 11. 13–24 ct	G	Judg. ch. 7 Luke 14. 25–end	Ezra ch. 6 Rom. 11. 13–24 ct
Ps. [52]; 53 Jer. 11. 1–14 Rom. 13. 1–10 *Gospel:* Luke 9. 51–end *or First EP of Thomas* Ps. 27 Isa. ch. 35 Heb. 10.35 – 11.1 **R** ct	**THE THIRD SUNDAY AFTER TRINITY** 2 Chron. 33. 9–13 Ps. 55. 17–23 1 Pet. 5. 5b–11 Luke 15. 1–10 G	Ps. 56 Deut. 15. 1–11 Acts 27. [13–32] 33–end	Ps. [52] 53 Jer. 11. 1–14 Rom. 13. 1–10
EP: Ps. 139 Job 42. 1–6 1 Pet. 1. 3–12		Judg. 8. 22–end Luke 15. 1–10	Ezra ch. 7 Rom. 11. 25–end
Ps. 72; 75 Ezra ch. 7 Rom. 11. 25–end	G		
Ps. 74 Ezra 8. 15–end Rom. 12. 1–8	**Translation of Martin, Bishop of Tours, c. 397** Com. Bishop Gw	Judg. 9. 1–21 Luke 15. 11–end	Ezra 8. 15–end Rom. 12. 1–8

July 2006

		Sunday Principal Service / Weekday Eucharist	Third Service / Morning Prayer

5 W / G
- Amos 5. 14–15, 21–24
- Ps. 50. 7–14
- Matt. 8. 28–end
- Ps. 77
- Judg. 9. 22–end
- Luke 16. 1–18

6 Th / G — *Thomas More, Scholar, and John Fisher, Bishop of Rochester, Reformation Martyrs, 1535*
- Amos 7. 10–end
- Ps. 19. 7–10
- Matt. 9. 1–8
- Ps. 78. 1–39†
- Judg. 11. 1–11
- Luke 16. 19–end

7 F* / G
- Amos 8. 4–6, 9–12
- Ps. 119. 1–8
- Matt. 9. 9–13
- Ps. 55
- Judg. 11. 29–end
- Luke 17. 1–10

8 Sa / G
- Amos 9. 11–end
- Ps. 85. 8–end
- Matt. 9. 14–17
- Ps. 76; 79
- Judg. 12. 1–7
- Luke 17. 11–19

9 S / G — THE FOURTH SUNDAY AFTER TRINITY (Proper 9)

Track 1
- 2 Sam. 5. 1–5, 9–10
- Ps. 48
- 2 Cor. 12. 2–10
- Mark 6. 1–13

Track 2
- Ezek. 2. 1–5
- Ps. 123
- 2 Cor. 12. 2–10
- Mark 6. 1–13

Third Service:
- Ps. 57
- Deut. 24. 10–end
- Acts 28. 1–16

10 M / G — DEL 14
- Hos. 2. 16–18, 21–22
- Ps. 145. 2–9
- Matt. 9. 18–26
- Ps. 80; 82
- Judg. 13. 1–24
- Luke 17. 20–end

11 Tu / Gw — **Benedict of Nursia, Abbot of Monte Cassino, Father of Western Monasticism, c. 550**
- Com. Religious
- also 1 Cor. 3. 10–11
- Luke 18. 18–22

or
- Hos. 8. 4–7, 11–13
- Ps. 103. 8–12
- Matt. 9. 32–end

Third Service:
- Ps. 87; 89. 1–18
- Judg. ch. 14
- Luke 18. 1–14

12 W / G
- Hos. 10. 1–3, 7–8, 12
- Ps. 115. 3–10
- Matt. 10. 1–7
- Ps. 119. 105–128
- Judg. 15. 1 – 16.3
- Luke 18. 15–30

13 Th / G
- Hos. 11. 1, 3–4, 8–9
- Ps. 105. 1–7
- Matt. 10. 7–15
- Ps. 90; 92
- Judg. 16. 4–end
- Luke 18. 31–end

14 F / Gw — **John Keble, Priest, Tractarian, Poet, 1866**
- Com. Pastor
- also Lam. 3. 19–26
- Matt. 5. 1–8

or
- Hos. 14. 2–end
- Ps. 80. 1–7
- Matt. 10. 16–23

Third Service:
- Ps. 88; (95)
- Judg. ch. 17
- Luke 19. 1–10

15 Sa / Gw — **Swithun, Bishop of Winchester, c. 862**
Bonaventure, Friar, Bishop, Teacher, 1274
- Com. Bishop
- also James 5. 7–11, 13–18

or
- Isa. 6. 1–8
- Ps. 51. 1–7
- Matt. 10. 24–33

Third Service:
- Ps. 96; 97; 100
- Judg. 18. 1–20, 27–end
- Luke 19. 11–27

16 S / G — THE FIFTH SUNDAY AFTER TRINITY (Proper 10)

Track 1
- 2 Sam. 6. 1–5, 12b–19
- Ps. 24
- Eph. 1. 3–14
- Mark 6. 14–29

Track 2
- Amos 7. 7–15
- Ps. 85. 8–end
- Eph. 1. 3–14
- Mark 6. 14–29

Third Service:
- Ps. 65
- Deut. 28. 1–14
- Acts 28. 17–end

17 M / G — DEL 15
- Isa. 1. 11–17
- Ps. 50. 7–15
- Matt. 10.34 – 11.1
- Ps. 98; 99; 101
- 1 Sam. 1. 1–20
- Luke 19. 28–40

18 Tu / G — *Elizabeth Ferard, first deaconess of the Church of England, Founder of the Community of St Andrew, 1883*
- Isa. 7. 1–9
- Ps. 48. 1–7
- Matt. 11. 20–24
- Ps. 106† (or 103)
- 1 Sam. 1.21 – 2.11
- Luke 19. 41–end

---

*Thomas Becket may be celebrated on 7 July instead of 29 December.

Second Service Evening Prayer	Calendar and Holy Communion	Morning Prayer	Evening Prayer
Ps. 119. 81–104 Ezra ch. 9 Rom. 12. 9–end	G	Judg. 9. 22–end Luke 16. 1–18	Ezra ch. 9 Rom. 12. 9–end
Ps. 78. 40–end† Ezra 10. 1–17 Rom. 13. 1–7	G	Judg. 11. 1–11 Luke 16. 19–end	Ezra 10. 1–17 Rom. 13. 1–7
Ps. 69 Neh. ch. 1 Rom. 13. 8–end	G	Judg. 11. 29–end Luke 17. 1–10	Neh. ch. 1 Rom. 13. 8–end
Ps. 81; *84* Neh. ch. 2 Rom. 14. 1–12 **ct**	G	Judg. 12. 1–7 Luke 17. 11–19	Neh. ch. 2 Rom. 14. 1–12 **ct**
	THE FOURTH SUNDAY AFTER TRINITY		
Ps. [63] 64 Jer. 20. 1–11a Rom. 14. 1–17 *Gospel:* Luke 10. 1–11, 16–20	Gen. 3. 17–19 Ps. 79. 8–10 Rom. 8. 18–23 Luke 6. 36–42 G	Ps. 57 Deut. 24. 10–22 Acts 28. 1–16	Ps. [63]; 64 Jer. 20. 1–11a Rom. 14. 1–17
Ps. *85*; 86 Neh. ch. 4 Rom. 14. 13–end	G	Judg. 13. 1–24 Luke 17. 20–end	Neh. ch. 4 Rom. 14. 13–end
Ps. 89. 19–end Neh. ch. 5 Rom. 15. 1–13	G	Judg. ch. 14 Luke 18. 1–14	Neh. ch. 5 Rom. 15. 1–13
Ps. *91*; 93 Neh. 6.1 – 7.4 Rom. 15. 14–21	G	Judg. 15. 1 – 16.3 Luke 18. 15–30	Neh. 6.1 – 7.4 Rom. 15. 14–21
Ps. 94 Neh. 7.73b – 8.end Rom. 15. 22–end	G	Judg. 16. 4–end Luke 18. 31–end	Neh. 7.73b – 8.end Rom. 15. 22–end
Ps. 102 Neh. 9. 1–23 Rom. 16. 1–16	G	Judg. ch. 17 Luke 19. 1–10	Neh. 9. 1–23 Rom. 16. 1–16
	Swithun, Bishop of Winchester, *c.* 862		
Ps. 104 Neh. 9. 24–end Rom. 16. 17–end **ct**	Com. Bishop Gw	Judg. 18. 1–20, 27–end Luke 19. 11–27	Neh. 9. 24–end Rom. 16. 17–end **ct**
	THE FIFTH SUNDAY AFTER TRINITY		
Ps. 66. 1–8 [9–end] Job 4. 1; 5. 6–end *or* Ecclus. 4. 11–end Rom. 15. 14–29 *Gospel:* Luke 10. 25–37	1 Kings 19. 19–21 Ps. 84. 8–end 1 Pet. 3. 8–15a Luke 5. 1–11	Ps. 65 Deut. 28. 1–14 Acts 28. 17–end	Ps. 66. 1–8 [9–end] Job 4. 1; 5. 6–end *or* Ecclus. 4. 11–end Luke 10. 21–24
Ps. *105*† (*or* 103) Neh. 12. 27–47 2 Cor. 1. 1–14	G	1 Sam. 1. 1–20 Luke 19. 28–40	Neh. 12. 27–47 2 Cor. 1. 1–14
Ps. 107† Neh. 13. 1–14 2 Cor. 1.15 – 2.4	G	1 Sam. 1.21 – 2.11 Luke 19. 41–end	Neh. 13. 1–14 2 Cor. 1.15 – 2.4

July 2006

Sunday Principal Service
Weekday Eucharist

Third Service
Morning Prayer

19	W	**Gregory, Bishop of Nyssa, and his sister Macrina, Deaconess, Teachers, *c.* 394 and *c.* 379**		
		Com. Teacher *or*	Isa. 10. 5–7, 13–16	110; *111*; 112
		esp. 1 Cor. 2. 9–13	Ps. 94. 5–11	1 Sam. 2. 12–26
	Gw	*also* Wisd. 9. 13–17	Matt. 11. 25–27	Luke 20. 1–8
20	Th	*Margaret of Antioch, Martyr, 4th century; Bartolomé de las Casas, Apostle to the Indies, 1566*		
			Isa. 26. 7–9, 16–19	Ps. 113; *115*
			Ps. 102. 14–21	1 Sam. 2. 27–end
	G		Matt. 11. 28–end	Luke 20. 9–19
21	F		Isa. 38. 1–6, 21–22, 7–8	Ps. 139
			Canticle: Isa. 38. 10–16	1 Sam. 3.1 – 4.1a
			or Ps. 32. 1–8	Luke 20. 20–26
			Matt. 12. 1–8	
	G			
22	Sa	MARY MAGDALENE		
			Song of Sol. 3. 1–4	*MP:* Ps. 30; 32; 150
			Ps. 42. 1–7	1 Sam. 16. 14–end
			2 Cor. 5. 14–17	Luke 8. 1–3
	W		John 20. 1–2, 11–18	
23	S	THE SIXTH SUNDAY AFTER TRINITY (Proper 11)		
		Track 1	*Track 2*	
		2 Sam. 7. 1–14a	Jer. 23. 1–6	Ps. 67; 70
		Ps. 89. 20–37	Ps. 23	Deut. 30. 1–10
		Eph. 2. 11–end	Eph. 2. 11–end	1 Pet. 3. 8–18
		Mark 6. 30–34, 53–end	Mark 6. 30–34, 53–end	
	G			
24 DEL 16	M		Mic. 6. 1–4, 6–8	Ps. 123; 124; 125; *126*
			Ps. 50. 3–7, 14	1 Sam. ch. 5
			Matt. 12. 38–42	Luke 20. 41 – 21.4
	G			
25	Tu	JAMES THE APOSTLE		
		The reading from Acts must	Jer. 45. 1–5	*MP:* Ps. 7; 29; 117
		be used as either the first or	*or* Acts 11.27 – 12.2	2 Kings 1. 9–15
		second reading at the	Ps. 126	Luke 9. 46–56
		Principal Service	Acts 11.27 – 12.2	
			or 2 Cor. 4. 7–15	
	R		Matt. 20. 20–28	
26	W	**Anne and Joachim, Parents of the Blessed Virgin Mary**		
		Zeph. 3. 14–18a *or*	Jer. 1. 1, 4–10	Ps. 119. 153–end
		Ps. 127	Ps. 70	1 Sam. ch. 7
		Rom. 8. 28–30	Matt. 13. 1–9	Luke 21. 20–28
	Gw	Matt. 13. 16–17		
27	Th	*Brooke Foss Westcott, Bishop of Durham, Teacher, 1901*		
			Jer. 2. 1–3, 7–8, 12–13	Ps. *143*; 146
			Ps. 36. 5–10	1 Sam. ch. 8
	G		Matt. 13. 10–17	Luke 21. 29–end
28	F		Jer. 3. 14–17	Ps. 142; *144*
			Ps. 23	1 Sam. 9. 1–14
			or Canticle: Jer. 31. 10–13	Luke 22. 1–13
	G		Matt. 13. 18–23	
29	Sa	**Mary, Martha and Lazarus, Companions of our Lord**		
		Isa. 25. 6–9 *or*	Jer. 7. 1–11	Ps. 147
		Ps. 49. 1–10, 16	Ps. 84. 1–6	1 Sam. 9.15 – 10.1
		Heb. 2. 10–15	Matt. 13. 24–30	Luke 22. 14–23
	Gw	John 12. 1–8		

Second Service Evening Prayer	Calendar and Holy Communion	Morning Prayer	Evening Prayer
Ps. 119. 129–152 Neh. 13. 15–end 2 Cor. 2. 5–end	G	1 Sam. 2. 12–26 Luke 20. 1–8	Neh. 13. 15–end 2 Cor. 2. 5–end
Ps. 114; *116*; 117 Esther ch. 1 2 Cor. ch. 3	**Margaret of Antioch, Martyr, 4th century** Com. Virgin Martyr Gr	1 Sam. 2. 27–end Luke 20. 9–19	Esther ch. 1 2 Cor. ch. 3
Ps. *130*; 131; 137 Esther ch. 2 2 Cor. ch. 4 *or First EP of Mary Magdalene* Ps. 139 Isa. 25. 1–9 2 Cor. 1. 3–7 **W ct**	G	1 Sam. 3.1 – 4.1a Luke 20. 20–26	Esther ch. 2 2 Cor. ch. 4 *or First EP of Mary Magdalene* (Ps. 139) Isa. 25. 1–9 2 Cor. 1. 3–7 **W ct**
EP: Ps. 63 Zeph. 3. 14–20 Mark 15.40 – 16.7	**MARY MAGDALENE** Zeph. 3. 14–end Ps. 30. 1–5 2 Cor. 5. 14–17 John 20. 11–18 W	(Ps. 30; 32; 150) 1 Sam. 16. 14–end Luke 8. 1–3	(Ps. 63) Song of Sol. 3. 1–4 Mark 15.40 – 16.7
Ps. 73. [1–20] 21–end Job 13.13 – 14.6 *or Ecclus.* 18. 1–14 Heb. 2. 5–end *Gospel:* Luke 10. 38–end	**THE SIXTH SUNDAY AFTER TRINITY** Gen. 4. 2b–15 Ps. 90. 12–end Rom. 6. 3–11 Matt. 5. 20–26 G	Ps. 67; 70 Deut. 30. 1–10 1 Pet. 3. 13–22	Ps. 73. [1–20] 21–end Job 13.13 – 14.6 *or Ecclus.* 18. 1–14 Heb. 2. 5–end
Ps. *127*; 128; 129 Esther ch. 4 2 Cor. 6.1 – 7.1 *or First EP of James* Ps. 144 Deut. 30. 11–end Mark 5. 21–end **R ct**	G	1 Sam. ch. 5 Luke 20. 41 – 21.4	Esther ch. 4 2 Cor. 6.1 – 7.1 *or First EP of James* (Ps. 144) Deut. 30. 11–end Mark 5. 21–end **R ct**
EP: Ps. 94 Jer. 26. 1–15 Mark 1. 14–20	**JAMES THE APOSTLE** 2 Kings 1. 9–15 Ps. 15 Acts 11.27 – 12.3a Matt. 20. 20–28 R	(Ps. 7; 29; 117) Jer. 45. 1–5 Luke 9. 46–56	(Ps. 94) Jer. 26. 1–15 Mark 1. 14–20
Ps. 136 Esther 6. 1–13 2 Cor. 8. 1–15	**Anne, Mother of the Blessed Virgin Mary** Com. Saint Gw	1 Sam. ch. 7 Luke 21. 20–28	Esther 6. 1–13 2 Cor. 8. 1–15
Ps. *138*; 140; 141 Esther 6.14 – 7.end 2 Cor. 8.16 – 9.5	G	1 Sam. ch. 8 Luke 21. 29–end	Esther 6.14 – 7.end 2 Cor. 8.16 – 9.5
Ps. 145 Esther ch. 8 2 Cor. 9. 6–end	G	1 Sam. 9. 1–14 Luke 22. 1–13	Esther ch. 8 2 Cor. 9. 6–end
Ps. *148*; 149; 150 Esther 9. 20–28 2 Cor. ch. 10 ct	G	1 Sam. 9.15 – 10.1 Luke 22. 14–23	Esther 9. 20–28 2 Cor. ch. 10 ct

July 2006

		Sunday Principal Service Weekday Eucharist	Third Service Morning Prayer

30 S

THE SEVENTH SUNDAY AFTER TRINITY (Proper 12)

Track 1	*Track 2*	
2 Sa. 11. 1–15	2 Kings 4. 42–end	Ps. 75
Ps. 14	Ps. 145. 10–19	Song of Sol. ch. 2
Eph. 3. 14–end	Eph. 3. 14–end	*or* 1 Macc. 2. [1–14] 15–22
G John 6. 1–21	John 6. 1–21	1 Pet. 4. 7–14

31 M
DEL 17

Ignatius of Loyola, Founder of the Society of Jesus, 1556

	Jer. 13. 1–11	Ps. *1*; 2; 3
	Ps. 82	1 Sam. 10. 1–16
	or Deut. 32. 18–21	Luke 22. 24–30
G	Matt. 13. 31–35	

August 2006

1 Tu

	Jer. 14. 17–end	Ps. *5*; 6; (8)
	Ps. 79. 8–end	1 Sam. 10. 17–end
G	Matt. 13. 36–43	Luke 22. 31–38

2 W

	Jer. 15. 10, 16–end	Ps. 119. 1–32
	Ps. 59. 1–4, 18–end	1 Sam. ch. 11
G	Matt. 13. 44–46	Luke 22. 39–46

3 Th

	Jer. 18. 1–6	Ps. 14; *15*; 16
	Ps. 146. 1–5	1 Sam. ch. 12
G	Matt. 13. 47–53	Luke 22. 47–62

4 F

John-Baptiste Vianney, Curé d'Ars, Spiritual Guide, 1859

	Jer. 26. 1–9	Ps. 17; *19*
	Ps. 69. 4–10	1 Sam. 13. 5–18
G	Matt. 13. 54–end	Luke 22. 63–end

5 Sa

Oswald, King of Northumbria, Martyr, 642

Com. Martyr	*or* Jer. 26. 11–16, 24	Ps. 20; 21; *23*
esp. 1 Pet. 4. 12–end	Ps. 69. 14–20	1 Sam. 13.19 – 14.15
John 16. 29–33	Matt. 14. 1–12	Luke 23. 1–12

Gr

6 S

THE TRANSFIGURATION OF OUR LORD (*or* transferred to 7th)

	Dan. 7. 9–10, 13–14	*MP*: Ps. 27; 150
	Ps. 97	Ecclus. 48. 1–10
	2 Pet. 1. 16–19	*or* 1 Kings 19. 1–16
ℬ	Luke 9. 28–36	1 John 3. 1–3

or, for The Eighth Sunday after Trinity (Proper 13):

Track 1	*Track 2*	
2 Sam. 11.26 – 12.13a	Exod. 16. 2–4, 9–15	Ps. 86
Ps. 51. 1–13	Ps. 78. 23–29	Song of Sol. 5. 2–end
Eph. 4. 1–16	Eph. 4. 1–16	*or* 1 Macc. 3. 1–12
G John 6. 24–35	John 6. 24–35	2 Pet. 1. 1–15

7 M
DEL 18

For The Transfiguration of Our Lord, see 6th.

John Mason Neale, Priest, Hymn Writer, 1866

	Jer. ch. 28	Ps. 27; *30*
	Ps. 119. 89–96	1 Sam. 14. 24–46
G	Matt. 14. 13–21 *or* 14. 22–end	Luke 23. 13–25

8 Tu

Dominic, Priest, Founder of the Order of Preachers, 1221

Com. Religious	*or* Jer. 30. 1–2, 12–15, 18–22	Ps. 32; *36*
also Ecclus. 39. 1–10	Ps. 102. 16–21	1 Sam. 15. 1–23
	Matt. 14. 22–end	Luke 23. 26–43
Gw	*or* 15. 1–2, 10–14	

Second Service Evening Prayer	Calendar and Holy Communion	Morning Prayer	Evening Prayer
	THE SEVENTH SUNDAY AFTER TRINITY		
Ps. 74. [1–10] 11–16	1 Kings 17. 8–16	Ps. 75	Ps. 74. [1.11] 12–17
Job 19. 1–27	Ps. 34. 11–end	Song of Sol. ch. 2	Job 19. 1–27a
or Ecclus. 38. 24–end	Rom. 6. 19–end	*or* 1 Macc. 2. [1–14]	*or* Ecclus. 38. 24–end
Heb. ch. 8	Mark 8. 1–10a	15–22	Heb. ch. 8
Gospel: Luke 11. 1–13 G		1 Pet. 4. 7–14	
Ps. *4*; 7		1 Sam. 10. 1–16	Jer. ch. 26
Jer. ch. 26		Luke 22. 24–30	2 Cor. 11. 1–15
2 Cor. 11. 1–15			
G			
	Lammas Day		
Ps. *9*; 10†		1 Sam. 10. 17–end	Jer. ch. 28
Jer. ch. 28		Luke 22. 31–38	2 Cor. 11. 16–end
2 Cor. 11. 16–end G			
Ps. *11*; 12; 13		1 Sam. ch. 11	Jer. 29. 1–14
Jer. 29. 1–14		Luke 22. 39–46	2 Cor. ch. 12
2 Cor. ch. 12 G			
Ps. 18†		1 Sam. ch. 12	Jer. 30. 1–11
Jer. 30. 1–11		Luke 22. 47–62	2 Cor. ch. 13
2 Cor. ch. 13 G			
Ps. 22		1 Sam. 13. 5–18	Jer. 30. 12–22
Jer. 30. 12–22		Luke 22. 63–end	James 1. 1–11
James 1. 1–11 G			
Ps. *24*; 25		1 Sam. 13.19 – 14.15	Jer. 31. 1–22
Jer. 31. 1–22		Luke 23. 1–12	James 1. 12–end
James 1. 12–end			ct
ct			
or First EP of The			*or First EP of The*
Transfiguration			*Transfiguration*
Ps. 99; 110			(Ps. 99; 110)
Exod. 24. 12–end			Exod. 24. 12–end
John 12. 27–36a			John 12. 27–36a
℈ ct G			℈ ct
	THE TRANSFIGURATION OF OUR LORD (*or* transferred to 7th)		
EP: Ps. 72	Exod. 24. 12–end	Ps. 27; 150	Ps. 72
Exod. 34. 29–end	Ps. 84. 1–7	Ecclus. 48. 1–10	Exod. 34. 29–end
2 Cor. ch. 3	1 John 3. 1–3	*or* 1 Kings 19. 1–16	2 Cor. ch. 3
	Mark 9. 2–7	2 Pet. 1. 16–19	
℈			
	or, for the Eighth Sunday after Trinity:		
Ps. 88. 1–10 [11–end]	Jer. 23. 16–24	Ps. 86	Ps. 88. 1–10 [11–end]
Job ch. 28	Ps. 31. 1–6	Song of Sol. 5. 2–end	Job ch. 28
or Ecclus. 42. 15–end	Rom. 8. 12–17	*or* 1 Macc. 3. 1–12	*or* Ecclus. 42. 15–end
Heb. 11. 17–31	Matt. 7. 15–21	2 Pet. 1. 1–15	Heb. 11. 17–31
Gospel: Luke 12. 13–21 G			
	For the Transfiguration of Our Lord, see 6th.		
	The Name of Jesus		
Ps. 26; *28*; 29	Jer. 14. 7–9	1 Sam. 14. 24–46	Jer. 31. 23–25, 27–37
Jer. 31. 23–25, 27–37	Ps. 8	Luke 23. 13–25	James 2. 1–13
James 2. 1–13	Acts 4. 8–12		
Gw Matt. 1. 20–23			
Ps. 33		1 Sam. 15. 1–23	Jer. 32. 1–15
Jer. 32. 1–15		Luke 23. 26–43	James 2. 14–end
James 2. 14–end			
G			

August 2006

			Sunday Principal Service Weekday Eucharist		Third Service Morning Prayer

9 W — **Mary Sumner, Founder of the Mothers' Union, 1921**
Com. Saint *or* Jer. 31. 1–7 — Ps. 34
also Heb. 13. 1–5 — Ps. 121 — 1 Sam. ch. 16
Gw — Matt. 15. 21–28 — Luke 23. 44–56a

10 Th — **Laurence, Deacon at Rome, Martyr, 258**
Com. Martyr *or* Jer. 31. 31–34 — Ps. 37†
also 2 Cor. 9. 6–10 — Ps. 51. 11–18 — 1 Sam. 17. 1–30
Gr — Matt. 16. 13–23 — Luke 23.56b – 24.12

11 F — **Clare of Assisi, Founder of the Minoresses (Poor Clares), 1253**
John Henry Newman, Priest, Tractarian, 1890
Com. Religious *or* Nahum 2. 1, 3; 3. 1, 6–7 — Ps. 31
esp. Song of Sol. 8. 6–7 — Ps. 137. 1–6 — 1 Sam. 17. 31–54
or Deut. 32. 35–36, 39, 41 — Luke 24. 13–35
Gw — Matt. 16. 24–28

12 Sa — — Hab. 1.12 – 2.4 — Ps. 41; *42*; 43
Ps. 9. 7–11 — 1 Sam. 17.55 – 18.16
G — Matt. 17. 14–20 — Luke 24. 36–end

13 S — THE NINTH SUNDAY AFTER TRINITY (Proper 14)
Track 1 — *Track 2*
2 Sam. 18. 5–9, 15, 31–33 — 1 Kings 19. 4–8 — Ps. 90
Ps. 130 — Ps. 34. 1–18 — Song of Sol. 8. 5–7
Eph. 4.25 – 5.2 — Eph. 4.25 – 5.2 — *or* 1 Macc. 14. 4–15
John 6. 35, 41–51 — John 6. 35, 41–51 — 2 Pet. 3. 8–13
G

14 M — *Maximilian Kolbe, Friar, Martyr, 1941*
DEL 19 — Ezek. 1. 2–5, 24–end — Ps. 44
Ps. 148. 1–4, 12–13a — 1 Sam. 19. 1–18
Matt. 17. 22–end — Acts 1. 1–14

15 Tu
G — THE BLESSED VIRGIN MARY* — Isa. 61. 10–end — *MP:* Ps. 98; 138; 147. 1–12
or Rev. 11.19 – 12.6, 10 — Isa. 7. 10–15
Ps. 45. 10–end — Luke 11. 27–28
Gal. 4. 4–7
W — Luke 1. 46–55

or, if The Blessed Virgin — Ezek. 2.8 – 3.4 — Ps. *48*; 52
Mary is celebrated on — Ps. 119. 65–72 — 1 Sam. 20. 1–17
8 September: — Matt. 18. 1–5, 10, — Acts 1. 15–end
G — 12–14

16 W — — Ezek. 9. 1–7, 10, 18–22 — Ps. 119. 57–80
Ps. 113 — 1 Sam. 20. 18–end
G — Matt. 18. 15–20 — Acts 2. 1–21

17 Th — — Ezek. 12. 1–12 — Ps. 56; *57* (63†)
Ps. 78. 58–64 — 1 Sam. 21.1 – 22.5
G — Matt. 18.21 – 19.1 — Acts 2. 22–36

18 F — — Ezek. 16. 1–15, 60–end — Ps. *51*; 54
Ps. 118. 14–18 — 1 Sam. 22. 6–end
G — Matt. 19. 3–12 — Acts 2. 37–end

19 Sa — — Ezek. 18. 1–10, 13, 30, 32 — Ps. 68
Ps. 51. 1–3, 15–17 — 1 Sam. ch. 23
G — Matt. 19. 13–15 — Acts 3. 1–10

*The Blessed Virgin Mary may be celebrated on 8 September instead of 15 August.

Second Service Evening Prayer	Calendar and Holy Communion		Morning Prayer	Evening Prayer
Ps. 119. 33–56 Jer. 33. 1–13 James ch. 3		G	1 Sam. ch. 16 Luke 23. 44–56a	Jer. 33. 1–13 James ch. 3
Ps. 39; *40* Jer. 33. 14–end James 4. 1–12	**Laurence, Deacon at Rome, Martyr, 258** Com. Martyr	Gr	1 Sam. 17. 1–30 Luke 23.56b – 24.12	Jer. 33. 14–end James 4. 1–12
Ps. 35 Jer. ch. 35 James 4.13 – 5.6		G	1 Sam. 17. 31–54 Luke 24. 13–35	Jer. ch. 35 James 4.13 – 5.6
Ps. 45; *46* Jer. 36. 1–18 James 5. 7–end ct		G	1 Sam. 17.55 – 18.16 Luke 24. 36–end	Jer. 36. 1–18 James 5. 7–end ct
	THE NINTH SUNDAY AFTER TRINITY			
Ps. 91. 1–12 [13–end] Job 39.1 – 40.4 *or* Ecclus. 43. 13–end Heb. 12. 1–17 *Gospel:* Luke 12. 32–40	Num. 10.35 – 11.3 Ps. 95 1 Cor. 10. 1–13 Luke 16. 1–9 *or* Luke 15. 11–end	G	Ps. 89. 1–18 Song of Sol. 8. 5–7 *or* 1 Macc. 14. 4–15 2 Pet. 3. 8–13	Ps. 91. 1–12 [13–end] Job 39.1 – 40.4 *or* Ecclus. 43. 13–end Heb. 12. 1–17
Ps. *47*; 49 Jer. 36. 19–end Mark 1. 1–13 *or First EP of The Blessed Virgin Mary* Ps. 72 Prov. 8. 22–31 John 19. 23–27 W ct		G	1 Sam. 19. 1–18 Acts 1. 1–14	Jer. 36. 19–end Mark 1. 1–13
EP: Ps. 132 Song of Sol. 2. 1–7 Acts 1. 6–14	To celebrate The Blessed Virgin Mary, see *Common Worship* provision. 1 Sam. 20. 1–17 Acts 1. 15–end		Jer. ch. 37 Mark 1. 14–20	
Ps. 50 Jer. ch. 37 Mark 1. 14–20		G		
Ps. *59*; 60 (67) Jer. 38. 1–13 Mark 1. 21–28		G	1 Sam. 20. 18–end Acts 2. 1–21	Jer. 38. 1–13 Mark 1. 21–28
Ps. 61; *62*; 64 Jer. 38. 14–end Mark 1. 29–end		G	1 Sam. 21.1 – 22.5 Acts 2. 22–36	Jer. 38. 14–end Mark 1. 29–end
Ps. 38 Jer. ch. 39 Mark 2. 1–12		G	1 Sam. 22. 6–end Acts 2. 37–end	Jer. ch. 39 Mark 2. 1–12
Ps. 65; *66* Jer. ch. 40 Mark 2. 13–22 ct		G	1 Sam. ch. 23 Acts 3. 1–10	Jer. ch. 40 Mark 2. 13–22 ct

August 2006

	Sunday Principal Service / Weekday Eucharist	Third Service / Morning Prayer

20 S

THE TENTH SUNDAY AFTER TRINITY (Proper 15)

Track 1	Track 2	
1 Kings 2. 10–12; 3. 3–14	Prov. 9. 1–6	Ps. 106. 1–10
Ps. 111	Ps. 34. 9–14	Jonah ch. 1
Eph. 5. 15–20	Eph. 5. 15–20	or Ecclus. 3. 1–15
John 6. 51–58	John 6. 51–58	2 Pet. 3. 14–end

G

21 M
DEL 20

	Ezek. 24. 15–24	Ps. 71
	Ps. 78. 1–8	1 Sam. ch. 24
	Matt. 19. 16–22	Acts 3. 11–end

G

22 Tu

	Ezek. 28. 1–10	Ps. 73
	Ps. 107. 1–3, 40, 43	1 Sam. ch. 26
	Matt. 19. 23–end	Acts 4. 1–12

G

23 W

	Ezek. 34. 1–11	Ps. 77
	Ps. 23	1 Sam. 28. 3–end
	Matt. 20. 1–16	Acts 4. 13–31

G

24 Th

BARTHOLOMEW THE APOSTLE

The reading from Acts must be used as either the first or second reading at the Eucharist.	Isa. 43. 8–13	MP: Ps. 86; 117
	or Acts 5. 12–16	Gen. 28. 10–17
	Ps. 145. 1–7	John 1. 43–end
	Acts 5. 12–16	
	or 1 Cor. 4. 9–15	
	Luke 22. 24–30	

R

25 F

	Ezek. 37. 1–14	Ps. 55
	Ps. 107. 1–8	2 Sam. ch. 1
	Matt. 22. 34–40	Acts 5. 12–26

G

26 Sa

	Ezek. 43. 1–7	Ps. 76; 79
	Ps. 85. 7–end	2 Sam. 2. 1–11
	Matt. 23. 1–12	Acts 5. 27–end

G

27 S

THE ELEVENTH SUNDAY AFTER TRINITY (Proper 16)

Track 1	Track 2	
1 Kings 8. [1, 6, 10–11]22–30, 41–43	Josh. 24. 1–2a, 14–18	Ps. 115
Ps. 84	Ps. 34. 15–end	Jonah ch. 2
Eph. 6. 10–20	Eph. 6. 10–20	or Ecclus. 3. 17–29
John 6. 56–69	John 6. 56–69	Rev. ch. 1

G

28 M
DEL 21

Augustine, Bishop of Hippo, Teacher, 430

Com. Teacher	or 2 Thess. 1. 1–5, 11–12	Ps. 80; 82
esp. Ecclus. 39. 1–10	Ps. 39. 1–9	2 Sam. 3. 12–end
also Rom. 13. 11–13	Matt. 23. 13–22	Acts ch. 6

Gw

29 Tu

The Beheading of John the Baptist

Jer. 1. 4–10	or 2 Thess. 2. 1–3a, 14–17	Ps. 87; 89. 1–18
Ps. 11	Ps. 98	2 Sam. 5. 1–12
Heb. 11.32 – 12.2	Matt. 23. 23–26	Acts 7. 1–16
Matt. 14. 1–12		

Gr

30 W

John Bunyan, Spiritual Writer, 1688

Com. Teacher	or 2 Thess. 3. 6–10, 16–18	Ps. 119. 105–128
also Heb. 12. 1–2	Ps. 128	2 Sam. 6. 1–19
Luke 21. 21, 34–36	Matt. 23. 27–32	Acts 7. 17–43

Gw

31 Th

Aidan, Bishop of Lindisfarne, Missionary, 651

Com. Missionary	or 1 Cor. 1. 1–9	Ps. 90; 92
also 1 Cor. 9. 16–19	Ps. 145. 1–7	2 Sam. 7. 1–17
	Matt. 24. 42–end	Acts 7. 44–53

Gw

Second Service Evening Prayer		Calendar and Holy Communion	Morning Prayer	Evening Prayer
		THE TENTH SUNDAY AFTER TRINITY		
Ps. [92] 100 Exod. 2.23 – 3.10 Heb. 13. 1–15 *Gospel:* Luke 12. 49–56	G	Jer. 7. 9–15 Ps. 17. 1–8 1 Cor. 12. 1–11 Luke 19. 41–47a	Ps. 106. 1–10 Jonah ch. 1 *or* Ecclus. 3. 1–15 2 Pet. 3. 14–end	Ps. [92] 100 Exod. 2.23 – 3.10 Heb. 13. 1–15
Ps. 72; 75 Jer. ch. 41 Mark 2.23 – 3.6	G		1 Sam. ch. 24 Acts 3. 11–end	Jer. ch. 41 Mark 2.23 – 3.6
Ps. 74 Jer. ch. 42 Mark 3. 7–19a	G		1 Sam. ch. 26 Acts 4. 1–12	Jer. ch. 42 Mark 3. 7–19a
Ps. 119. 81–104 Jer. ch. 43 Mark 3. 19b–end *or First EP of Bartholomew* Ps. 97 Isa. 61. 1–9 2 Cor. 6. 1–10 **R ct**	G		1 Sam. 28. 3–end Acts 4. 13–31	Jer. ch. 43 Mark 3. 19b–end *or First EP of Bartholomew* (Ps. 97) Isa. 61. 1–9 2 Cor. 6. 1–10 **R ct**
		BARTHOLOMEW THE APOSTLE		
EP: Ps. 91; 116 Ecclus. 39. 1–10 *or* Deut. 18. 15–19 Matt. 10. 1–22	R	Gen. 28. 10–17 Ps. 15 Acts 5. 12–16 Luke 22. 24–30	(Ps. 86; 117) Isa. 43. 8–13 John 1. 43–end	(Ps. 91; 116) Ecclus. 39. 1–10 *or* Deut. 18. 15–19 Matt. 10. 1–22
Ps. 69 Jer. 44. 15–end Mark 4. 21–34	G		2 Sam. ch. 1 Acts 5. 12–26	Jer. 44. 15–end Mark 4. 21–34
Ps. 81; *84* Jer. ch. 45 Mark 4. 35–end **ct**	G		2 Sam. 2. 1–11 Acts 5. 27–end	Jer. ch. 45 Mark 4. 35–end **ct**
		THE ELEVENTH SUNDAY AFTER TRINITY		
Ps. 116. [1–9] 10–end Exod. 4.27 – 5.1 Heb. 13. 16–21 *Gospel:* Luke 13. 10–17	G	1 Kings 3. 5–15 Ps. 28 1 Cor. 15. 1–11 Luke 18. 9–14	Ps. 115 Jonah ch. 2 *or* Ecclus. 3. 17–29 Rev. ch. 1	Ps. 116. [1–9] 10–end Exod. 4.27 – 5.1 Heb. 13. 16–21
Ps. *85*; 86 Mic. 1. 1–9 Mark 5. 1–20	Gw	**Augustine, Bishop of Hippo, 430** Com. Doctor	2 Sam. 3. 12–end Acts ch. 6	Mic. 1. 1–9 Mark 5. 1–20
Ps. 89. 19–end Mic. ch. 2 Mark 5. 21–34	Gr	**The Beheading of John the Baptist** 2 Chron. 24. 17–21 Ps. 92. 11–end Heb. 11.32 – 12.2 Matt. 14. 1–12	2 Sam. 5. 1–12 Acts 7. 1–16	Mic. ch. 2 Mark 5. 21–34
Ps. *91*; 93 Mic. ch. 3 Mark 5. 35–end	G		2 Sam. 6. 1–19 Acts 7. 17–43	Mic. ch. 3 Mark 5. 35–end
Ps. 94 Mic. 4.1 – 5.1 Mark 6. 1–13	G		2 Sam. 7. 1–17 Acts 7. 44–53	Mic. 4.1 – 5.1 Mark 6. 1–13

September 2006

	Sunday Principal Service / Weekday Eucharist	Third Service / Morning Prayer

1 F — *Giles of Provence, Hermit, c. 710*
- 1 Cor. 1. 17–25
- Ps. 33. 6–12
- G — Matt. 25. 1–13

Ps. *88*; (95)
2 Sam. 7. 18–end
Acts 7.54 – 8.3

2 Sa — *The Martyrs of Papua New Guinea, 1901 and 1942*
- 1 Cor. 1. 26–end
- Ps. 33. 12–15, 20–end
- G — Matt. 25. 14–30

Ps. 96; *97*; 100
2 Sam. ch. 9
Acts 8. 4–25

3 S — **THE TWELFTH SUNDAY AFTER TRINITY (Proper 17)**

Track 1	Track 2	
Song of Sol. 2. 8–13	Deut. 4. 1–2, 6–9	Ps. 119. 17–40
Ps. 45. 1–2, 6–9 (*or* 1–7)	Ps. 15	Jonah 3. 1–9
James 1. 17–end	James 1. 17–end	*or* Ecclus. 11. [7–18]19–28
Mark 7. 1–8, 14–15, 21–23	Mark 7. 1–8, 14–15, 21–23	Rev. 3. 14–end

G

4 M — *Birinus, Bishop of Dorchester (Oxon), Apostle of Wessex, 650**
DEL 22
- 1 Cor. 2. 1–5
- Ps. 33. 12–21
- G — Luke 4. 16–30

Ps. *98*; 99; 101
2 Sam. ch. 11
Acts 8. 26–end

5 Tu
- 1 Cor. 2. 10–end
- Ps. 145. 10–17
- G — Luke 4. 31–37

Ps. *106*† (*or* 103)
2 Sam. 12. 1–25
Acts 9. 1–19a

6 W — *Allen Gardiner, Missionary, Founder of the South American Missionary Society, 1851*
- 1 Cor. 3. 1–9
- Ps. 62
- G — Luke 4. 38–end

Ps. 110; *111*; 112
2 Sam. 15. 1–12
Acts 9. 19b–31

7 Th
- 1 Cor. 3. 18–end
- Ps. 24. 1–6
- G — Luke 5. 1–11

Ps. 113; *115*
2 Sam. 15. 13–end
Acts 9. 32–end

8 F — **The Birth of the Blessed Virgin Mary****
Com. BVM　　*or*　1 Cor. 4. 1–5
- Ps. 37. 3–8
- Luke 5. 33–end
- Gw

Ps. 139
2 Sam. 16. 1–14
Acts 10. 1–16

9 Sa — *Charles Fuge Lowder, Priest, 1880*
- 1 Cor. 4. 6–15
- Ps. 145. 18–end
- Luke 6. 1–5
- G

Ps. 120; *121*; 122
2 Sam. 17. 1–23
Acts 10. 17–33

10 S — **THE THIRTEENTH SUNDAY AFTER TRINITY (Proper 18)**

Track 1	Track 2	
Prov. 22. 1–2, 8–9, 22–23	Isa. 35. 4–7a	Ps. 119. 57–72
Ps. 125	Ps. 146	Jonah 3.10 – 4.11
James 2. 1–10 [11–13] 14–17	James 2. 1–10 [11–13] 14–17	*or* Ecclus. 27.30 – 28.9
Mark 7. 24–end	Mark 7. 24–end	Rev. 8. 1–5

G

11 M
DEL 23
- 1 Cor. 5. 1–8
- Ps. 5. 5–9a
- G — Luke 6. 6–11

Ps. 123; 124; 125; *126*
2 Sam. 18. 1–18
Acts 10. 34–end

12 Tu
- 1 Cor. 6. 1–11
- Ps. 149. 1–5
- G — Luke 6. 12–19

Ps. *132*; 133
2 Sam 18.19 – 19.8a
Acts 11. 1–18

---

*Cuthbert may be celebrated on 4 September instead of 20 March, when the Common of a Missionary readings are used, *esp.* Ezek. 34. 11–16, *also* Matt. 18. 12–14.

**The Blessed Virgin Mary may be celebrated on 8 September instead of 15 August.

Second Service Evening Prayer	Calendar and Holy Communion	Morning Prayer	Evening Prayer
Ps. 102 Mic. 5. 2–end Mark 6. 14–29 **Gw**	**Giles of Provence, Hermit,** *c.* **710** Com. Abbot	2 Sam. 7. 18–end Acts 7.54 – 8.3	Mic. 5. 2–end Mark 6. 14–29
Ps. 104 Mic. ch. 6 Mark 6. 30–44 ct **G**		2 Sam. ch. 9 Acts 8. 4–25	Mic. ch. 6 Mark 6. 30–44 ct
	THE TWELFTH SUNDAY AFTER TRINITY		
Ps. 119. [1–8] 9–16 Exod. 12. 21–27 Matt. 4.23 – 5.20 **G**	Exod. 34. 29–end Ps. 34. 1–10 2 Cor. 3. 4–9 Mark 7. 31–37	Ps. 119. 17–40 Jonah 3. 1–9 *or* Ecclus. 11. [7–18] 19–28 Rev. 3. 14–end	Ps. 119. [1–8] 9–16 Exod. 12. 21–27 Matt. 4.23 – 5.20
Ps. *105*† (*or* 103) Mic. 7. 1–7 Mark 6. 45–end **G**		2 Sam. ch. 11 Acts 8. 26–end	Mic. 7. 1–7 Mark 6. 45–end
Ps. 107† Mic. 7. 8–end Mark 7. 1–13 **G**		2 Sam. 12. 1–25 Acts 9. 1–19a	Mic. 7. 8–end Mark 7. 1–13
Ps. 119. 129–152 Hab. 1. 1–11 Mark 7. 14–23 **G**		2 Sam. 15. 1–12 Acts 9. 19b–31	Hab. 1. 1–11 Mark 7. 14–23
Ps. 114; *116*; 117 Hab. 1.12 – 2.5 Mark 7. 24–30 **Gw**	**Evurtius, Bishop of Orleans, 4th century** Com. Bishop	2 Sam. 15. 13–end Acts 9. 32–end	Hab. 1.12 – 2.5 Mark 7. 24–30
Ps. *130*; 131; 137 Hab. 2. 6–end Mark 7. 31–end **Gw**	**The Nativity of the Blessed Virgin Mary** Gen. 3. 9–15 Ps. 45. 11–18 Rom. 5. 12–17 Luke 11. 27–28	2 Sam. 16. 1–14 Acts 10. 1–16	Hab. 2. 6–end Mark 7. 31–end
Ps. 118 Hab. 3. 2–19a Mark 8. 1–10 ct **G**		2 Sam. 17. 1–23 Acts 10. 17–33	Hab. 3. 2–19a Mark 8. 1–10 ct
	THE THIRTEENTH SUNDAY AFTER TRINITY		
Ps. 119. [41–48] 49–56 Exod. 14. 5–end Matt. 6. 1–18 **G**	Lev. 19. 13–18 Ps. 74. 20–end Gal. 3. 16–22 *or* Heb. 13. 1–6 Luke 10. 23b–37	Ps. 119. 57–72 Jonah 3.10 – 4.11 *or* Ecclus. 27.30 – 28.9 Rev. 8. 1–5	Ps. 119. [41–48] 49–56 Exod. 14. 5–end Matt. 6. 1–18
Ps. *127*; 128; 129 Hag. 1. 1–11 Mark 8. 11–21 **G**		2 Sam. 18. 1–18 Acts 10. 34–end	Hag. 1. 1–11 Mark 8. 11–21
Ps. (134); *135* Hag. 1.12 – 2.9 Mark 8. 22–26 **G**		2 Sam 18.19 – 19.8a Acts 11. 1–18	Hag. 1.12 – 2.9 Mark 8. 22–26

September 2006

13 W **John Chrysostom, Bishop of Constantinople, Teacher, 407**
Com. Teacher *or* 1 Cor. 7. 25–31
esp. Matt. 5. 13–19   Ps. 45. 11–end
also Jer. 1. 4–10   Luke 6. 20–26

Ps. 119. 153–end
2 Sam 19. 8b–23
Acts 11. 19–end

Gw

14 Th HOLY CROSS DAY

Num. 21. 4–9   *MP:* Ps. 2; 8; 146
Ps. 22. 23–28   Gen. 3. 1–15
Phil. 2. 6–11   John 12. 27–36a
R   John 3. 13–17

---

15 F **Cyprian, Bishop of Carthage, Martyr, 258**
Com. Martyr *or* 1 Cor. 9. 16–19, 22–end
esp. 1 Pet. 4. 12–end   Ps. 84. 1–6
Gr *also* Matt. 18. 18–22   Luke 6. 39–42

Ps. 142; *144*
2 Sam. 23. 1–7
Acts 12. 18–end

16 Sa **Ninian, Bishop of Galloway, Apostle of the Picts, *c.* 432**
Edward Bouverie Pusey, Priest, Tractarian, 1882
Com. Missionary *or* 1 Cor. 10. 14–22
esp. Acts 13. 46–49   Ps. 116. 10–end
Mark 16. 15–end   Luke 6. 43–end

Ps. 147
2 Sam. ch. 24
Acts 13. 1–12

Gw

17 S THE FOURTEENTH SUNDAY AFTER TRINITY (Proper 19)
Track 1   *Track 2*
Prov. 1. 20–33   Isa. 50. 4–9a
Ps. 19. 1–6 [7–end]   Ps. 116. 1–8
or Canticle: Wisd. 7.26 – 8.1   James 3. 1–12
James 3. 1–12   Mark 8. 27–end
G   Mark 8. 27–end

Ps. 119. 105–120
Isa. 44.24 – 45.8
Rev. 12. 1–12

18 M
DEL 24 G
1 Cor. 11. 17–26, 33
Ps. 40. 7–11
Luke 7. 1–10

Ps. *1*; 2; 3
1 Kings 1. 5–31
Acts 13. 13–43

19 Tu *Theodore of Tarsus, Archbishop of Canterbury, 690*
1 Cor. 12. 12–14, 27–end
Ps. 100
G   Luke 7. 11–17

Ps. *5*; 6; (8)
1 Kings 1.32 – 2.4, 10–12
Acts 13.44 – 14.7

20 W **John Coleridge Patteson, first Bishop of Melanesia and his Companions, Martyrs, 1871**
Com. Martyr *or* 1 Cor. 12.31b – 13.end
esp. 2 Chron. 24. 17–21   Ps. 33. 1–12
also Acts 7. 55–60   Luke 7. 31–35

Ps. 119. 1–32
1 Kings ch. 3
Acts 14. 8–end

Gr

21 Th MATTHEW, APOSTLE AND EVANGELIST
Prov. 3. 13–18   *MP:* Ps. 49; 117
Ps. 119. 65–72   1 Kings 19. 15–end
2 Cor. 4. 1–6   2 Tim. 3. 14–end
R   Matt. 9. 9–13

22 F
G
1 Cor. 15. 12–20
Ps. 17. 1–8
Luke 8. 1–3

Ps. 17; *19*
1 Kings 6. 1, 11–28
Acts 15. 22–35

23 Sa
G
1 Cor. 15. 35–37, 42–49
Ps. 30. 1–5
Luke 8. 4–15

Ps. 20; 21; *23*
1 Kings 8. 1–30
Acts 15.36 – 16.5

Second Service Evening Prayer	Calendar and Holy Communion	Morning Prayer	Evening Prayer
Ps. 136 Hag. 2. 10–end Mark 8.27 – 9.1 *or First EP of Holy Cross Day* Ps. 66 Isa. 52.13 – 53.end Eph. 2. 11–end R ct	G	2 Sam 19. 8b–23 Acts 11. 19–end	Hag. 2. 10–end Mark 8.27 – 9.1
EP: Ps. 110; 150 Isa. 63. 1–16 1 Cor. 1. 18–25	**Holy Cross Day** To celebrate Holy Cross as a festival, see *Common Worship* provision. Num. 21. 4–9 Ps. 67 1 Cor. 1. 17–25 **Gr** John 12. 27–33	2 Sam. 19. 24–end Acts 12. 1–17	Zech. 1. 1–17 Mark 9. 2–13
Ps. 145 Zech. 1.18 – 2.end Mark 9. 14–29	G	2 Sam. 23. 1–7 Acts 12. 18–end	Zech. 1.18 – 2.end Mark 9. 14–29
Ps. *148*; 149; 150 Zech. ch. 3 Mark 9. 30–37 ct	G	2 Sam. ch. 24 Acts 13. 1–12	Zech. ch. 3 Mark 9. 30–37 ct
	THE FOURTEENTH SUNDAY AFTER TRINITY		
Ps. 119. 73–80 [81–88] Exod. 18. 13–26 Matt. 7. 1–14	2 Kings 5. 9–16 Ps. 118. 1–9 Gal. 5. 16–24 Luke 17. 11–19 G	Ps. 119. 105–120 Isa. 44.24 – 45.8 Rev. 12. 1–12	Ps. 119. 73–80 [81–88] Exod. 18. 13–26 Matt. 7. 1–14
Ps. *4*; 7 Zech. ch. 4 Mark 9. 38–end	G	1 Kings. 1, 5–31 Acts 13. 13–43	Zech. ch. 4 Mark 9. 38–end
Ps. *9*; 10† Zech. 6. 9–end Mark 10. 1–16	G	1 Kings. 1.32 – 2.4, 10–12 Acts 13.44 – 14.7	Zech. 6. 9–end Mark 10. 1–16
Ps. *11*; 12; 13 Zech. ch. 7 Mark 10. 17–31 *or First EP of Matthew* Ps. 34 Isa. 33. 13–17 Matt. 6. 19–end R ct	G	1 Kings ch. 3 Acts 14. 8–end	Zech. ch. 7 Mark 10. 17–31 *or First EP of Matthew* (Ps. 34) Prov. 3. 3–18 Matt. 6. 19–end R ct
EP: Ps. 119. 33–40, 89–96 Eccles. 5. 4–12 Matt. 19. 16–end	MATTHEW, APOSTLE AND EVANGELIST Isa. 33. 13–17 Ps. 119. 65–72 2 Cor. 4. 1–6 **R** Matt. 9. 9–13	(Ps. 49; 117) 1 Kings 19. 15–end 2 Tim. 3. 14–end	(Ps. 119. 33–40, 89–96) Eccles. 5. 4–12 Matt. 19. 16–end
Ps. 22 Zech. 8. 9–end Mark 10. 35–45	G	1 Kings 6. 1, 11–28 Acts 15. 22–35	Zech. 8. 9–end Mark 10. 35–45
Ps. *24*; 25 Zech. 9. 1–12 Mark 10. 46–end ct	G	1 Kings 8. 1–30 Acts 15.36 – 16.5	Zech. 9. 1–12 Mark 10. 46–end ct

September 2006

		Sunday Principal Service Weekday Eucharist	Third Service Morning Prayer

24 S

THE FIFTEENTH SUNDAY AFTER TRINITY (Proper 20)

Track 1	*Track 2*	
Prov. 31. 10–end	Wisd. 1.16 – 2.1, 12–22	Ps. 119. 153–end
Ps. 1	*or* Jer. 11. 18–20	Isa. 45. 9–22
James 3.13 – 4.3, 7–8a	Ps. 54	Rev. 14. 1–5
Mark 9. 30–37	James 3.13 – 4.3, 7–8a	

G | | Mark 9. 30–37 |

25 M
DEL 25

Lancelot Andrewes, Bishop of Winchester, Spiritual Writer, 1626
Sergei of Radonezh, Russian Monastic Reformer, Teacher, 1392

Com. Bishop	*or* Prov. 3. 27–34	Ps. 27; *30*
esp. Isa. 6. 1–8	Ps. 15	1 Kings 8. 31–62
Gw	Luke 8. 16–18	Acts 16. 6–24

26 Tu

Wilson Carlile, Founder of the Church Army, 1942

	Prov. 21. 1–6, 10–13	Ps. 32; *36*
	Ps. 119. 1–8	1 Kings 8.63 – 9. 9
G	Luke 8. 19–21	Acts 16. 25–end

27 W

Vincent de Paul, Founder of the Congregation of the Mission (Lazarists), 1660
Ember Day*

Com. Religious	*or* Prov. 30. 5–9	Ps. 34
Gw *or*	*also* 1 Cor. 1. 25–end	Ps. 119. 105–112	1 Kings 10. 1–25
Rw	Matt. 25. 34–40	Luke 9. 1–6	Acts 17. 1–15

28 Th

	Eccles. 1. 2–11	Ps. 37†
	Ps. 90. 1–6	1 Kings 11. 1–13
	Luke 9. 7–9	Acts 17. 16–end

G

29 F

MICHAEL AND ALL ANGELS
Ember Day*

The reading from Revelation	Gen. 28. 10–17	*MP*: Ps. 34; 150
must be used as either the	*or* Rev. 12. 7–12	Tobit 12. 6–end
first or second reading at	Ps. 103. 19–end	*or* Dan. 12. 1–4
the Eucharist.	Rev. 12. 7–12	Acts 12. 1–11
	or Heb. 1. 5–end	
W	John 1. 47–end	

30 Sa

Ember Day*
Jerome, Translator of the Scriptures, Teacher, 420

	Eccles. 11.9 – 12.8	Ps. 41; *42*; 43
	Ps. 90. 1–2, 12–end	1 Kings 12. 1–24
	Luke 9. 43–45	Acts 18.22 – 19.7

G *or* R

October 2006

1 S

THE SIXTEENTH SUNDAY AFTER TRINITY (Proper 21)

Track 1	*Track 2*	
Esther 7. 1–6, 9–10; 9. 20–22	Num. 11. 4–6, 10–16, 24–29	Ps. 122
Ps. 124	Ps. 19. 7–end	Isa. 48. 12–end
James 5. 13–end	James 5. 13–end	Luke 11. 37–end
G	Mark 9. 38–end	Mark 9. 38–end	

or, if observed as Dedication Festival:

	Gen. 28. 11–18	*MP*: Ps. 48; 150
	or Rev. 21. 9–14	Hag. 2. 6–9
	Ps. 122	Heb. 10. 19–25
	1 Pet. 2. 1–10	
	John 10. 22–29	

ꟿ

---

*For Ember Day provision, see p. 13.

Second Service Evening Prayer	Calendar and Holy Communion	Morning Prayer	Evening Prayer
	THE FIFTEENTH SUNDAY AFTER TRINITY		
Ps. 119. 137–144 [145–152] Exod. 19. 10–end Matt. 8. 23–end	Josh. 24. 14–25 Ps. 92. 1–6 Gal. 6. 11–end Matt. 6. 24–end **G**	Ps. 119. 153–end Isa. 45. 9–22 Rev. 14. 1–5	Ps. 119. 137–144 [145–152] Exod. 19. 10–end Matt. 8. 23–end
Ps. 26; *28*; 29 Zech. ch. 10 Mark 11. 1–11	**G**	1 Kings 8. 31–62 Acts 16. 6–24	Zech. ch. 10 Mark 11. 1–11
Ps. 33 Zech. 11. 4–end Mark 11. 12–26	**Cyprian, Bishop of Carthage, Martyr, 258** Com. Martyr **Gr**	1 Kings 8.63 – 9. 9 Acts 16. 25–end	Zech. 11. 4–end Mark 11. 12–26
Ps. 119. 33–56 Zech. 12. 1–10 Mark 11. 27–end	Ember Day Ember CEG **G** or **R**	1 Kings 10. 1–25 Acts 17. 1–15	Zech. 12. 1–10 Mark 11. 27–end
Ps. 39; *40* Zech. ch. 13 Mark 12. 1–12 *or First EP of Michael and All Angels* Ps. 91 2 Kings 6. 8–17 Matt. 18. 1–6, 10 **W ct**	**G**	1 Kings 11. 1–13 Acts 17. 16–end	Zech. ch. 13 Mark 12. 1–12 *or First EP of Michael and All Angels* (Ps. 91) 2 Kings 6. 8–17 John 1. 47–51 **W ct**
EP: Ps. 138; 148 Dan. 10. 4–end Rev. ch. 5	**MICHAEL AND ALL ANGELS** Ember Day Ps. 103. 17–22 Dan. 10. 10–19a Rev. 12. 7–12 Matt. 18. 1–10 **W**	(Ps. 34; 150) Tobit 12. 6–end *or* Dan. 12. 1–4 Acts 12. 1–11	(Ps. 138; 148) Gen. 28. 10–17 Rev. ch. 5
Ps. 45; *46* Zech. 14. 12–end Mark 12. 18–27 **ct** *or First EP of Dedication Festival* Ps. 24 2 Chron. 7. 11–16 John 4. 19–29 **ẞ ct**	*Jerome, Translator of the Scriptures, Teacher, 420* Ember Day Ember CEG Com. Doctor **G** or **R**	1 Kings 12. 1–24 Acts 18.22 – 19.7	Zech. 14. 12–end Mark 12. 18–27 **ct** *or First EP of Dedication Festival* Ps. 24 2 Chron. 7. 11–16 John 4. 19–29 **ẞ ct**
	THE SIXTEENTH SUNDAY AFTER TRINITY		
Ps. 120; 121 Exod. ch. 24 Matt. 9. 1–8	1 Kings 17. 17–end Ps. 102. 12–17 Eph. 3. 13–end **G** Luke 7. 11–17 *or, if observed as Dedication Festival:*	Ps. 132 Isa. 48. 12–end Luke 11. 37–end	Ps. 120; 121 Exod. ch. 24 Matt. 9. 1–8
EP: Ps. 132 Jer. 7. 1–11 Luke 19. 1–10	2 Chron. 7. 11–16 Ps. 122 1 Cor. 3. 9–17 *or* 1 Pet. 2. 1–5 Matt. 21. 12–16 **ẞ** *or* John 10. 22–29	Ps. 132 Hag. 2. 6–9 Heb. 10. 19–25	Ps. 48; 150 Jer. 7. 1–11 Luke 19. 1–10

October 2006

		Sunday Principal Service Weekday Eucharist	Third Service Morning Prayer

2 M
DEL 26
G

Job 1. 6–end
Ps. 17. 1–11
Luke 9. 46–50

Ps. 44
1 Kings 12.25 – 13.10
Acts 19. 8–20

3 Tu
G

Job 3. 1–3, 11–17, 20–23
Ps. 88. 14–19
Luke 9. 51–56

Ps. 48; 52
1 Kings 13. 11–end
Acts 19. 21–end

4 W
Gw

Francis of Assisi, Friar, Deacon, Founder of the Friars Minor, 1226
Com. Religious   *or*   Job 9. 1–12, 14–16
also Gal. 6. 14–end   Ps. 88. 1–6, 11
Luke 12. 22–34   Luke 9. 57–end

Ps. 119. 57–80
1 Kings ch. 17
Acts 20. 1–16

5 Th
G

Job 19. 21–27a
Ps. 27. 13–16
Luke 10. 1–12

Ps. 56; 57 (63†)
1 Kings 18. 1–20
Acts 20. 17–end

6 F
Gr

William Tyndale, Translator of the Scriptures, Reformation Martyr, 1536
Com. Martyr   *or*   Job 38. 1, 12–21; 40. 3–5
also Prov. 8. 4–11   Ps. 139. 6–11
2 Tim. 3. 12–end   Luke 10. 13–16

Ps. 51; 54
1 Kings 18. 21–end
Acts 21. 1–16

7 Sa
G

Job 42. 1–3, 6, 12–end
Ps. 119. 169–end
Luke 10. 17–24

Ps. 68
1 Kings ch. 19
Acts 21. 17–36

8 S
G

THE SEVENTEENTH SUNDAY AFTER TRINITY (Proper 22)
Track 1   *Track 2*
Job 1. 1; 2. 1–10   Gen. 2. 18–24
Ps. 26   Ps. 8
Heb. 1. 1–4; 2. 5–12   Heb. 1. 1–4; 2. 5–12
Mark 10. 2–16   Mark 10. 2–16

Ps. 123; 124
Isa. 49. 13–23
Luke 12. 1–12

9 M
DEL 27
G

Denys, Bishop of Paris, and his Companions, Martyrs, c. 250; Robert Grosseteste, Bishop of Lincoln,
Philosopher, Scientist, 1253
Gal. 1. 6–12
Ps. 111. 1–6
Luke 10. 25–37

Ps. 71
1 Kings ch. 21
Acts 21.37 – 22.21

10 Tu
Gw

Paulinus, Bishop of York, Missionary, 644
Thomas Traherne, Poet, Spiritual Writer, 1674
Com. Missionary   *or*   Gal. 1. 13–end
esp. Matt. 28. 16–end   Ps. 139. 1–9
                                Luke 10. 38–end

Ps. 73
1 Kings 22. 1–28
Acts 22.22 – 23.11

11 W
G

Ethelburga, Abbess of Barking, 675; James the Deacon, Companion of Paulinus, 7th century
Gal. 2. 1–2, 7–14
Ps. 117
Luke 11. 1–4

Ps. 77
1 Kings 22. 29–45
Acts 23. 12–end

12 Th
Gw

Wilfrid of Ripon, Bishop, Missionary, 709
Elizabeth Fry, Prison Reformer, 1845; Edith Cavell, Nurse, 1915
Com. Missionary   *or*   Gal. 3. 1–5
esp. Luke 5. 1–11   *Canticle:* Benedictus
also 1 Cor. 1. 18–25   Luke 11. 5–13

Ps. 78. 1–39†
2 Kings 1. 2–17
Acts 24. 1–23

13 F
Gw

Edward the Confessor, King of England, 1066
Com. Saint   *or*   Gal. 3. 7–14
also 2 Sam. 23. 1–5   Ps. 111. 4–end
1 John 4. 13–16   Luke 11. 15–26

Ps. 55
2 Kings 2. 1–18
Acts 24.24 – 25.12

Second Service Evening Prayer	Calendar and Holy Communion	Morning Prayer	Evening Prayer
Ps. *47*; 49 Ecclus. 1. 1–10 *or* Ezek. 1. 1–14 Mark 12. 28–34 G		1 Kings 12.25 – 13.10 Acts 19. 8–20	Ecclus. 1. 1–10 *or* Ezek. 1. 1–14 Mark 12. 28–34
Ps. 50 Ecclus. 1. 11–end *or* Ezek. 1.15 – 2.2 Mark 12. 35–end G		1 Kings 13. 11–end Acts 19. 21–end	Ecclus. 1. 11–end *or* Ezek. 1.15 – 2.2 Mark 12. 35–end
Ps. *59*; 60 (67) Ecclus. ch. 2 *or* Ezek. 2.3 – 3.11 Mark 13. 1–13 G		1 Kings ch. 17 Acts 20. 1–16	Ecclus. ch. 2 *or* Ezek. 2.3 – 3.11 Mark 13. 1–13
Ps. 61; *62*; 64 Ecclus. 3. 17–29 *or* Ezek. 3. 12–end Mark 13. 14–23 G		1 Kings 18. 1–20 Acts 20. 17–end	Ecclus. 3. 17–29 *or* Ezek. 3. 12–end Mark 13. 14–23
Ps. 38 Ecclus. 4. 11–28 *or* Ezek. ch. 8 Mark 13. 24–31 Gr	**Faith of Aquitaine, Martyr, *c.* 304** Com. Virgin Martyr	1 Kings 18. 21–end Acts 21. 1–16	Ecclus. 4. 11–28 *or* Ezek. ch. 8 Mark 13. 24–31
Ps. 65; *66* Ecclus. 4.29 – 6.1 *or* Ezek. ch. 9 Mark 13. 32–end ct	G	1 Kings ch. 19 Acts 21. 17–36	Ecclus. 4.29 – 6.1 *or* Ezek. ch. 9 Mark 13. 32–end ct
	THE SEVENTEENTH SUNDAY AFTER TRINITY		
Ps. 125; 126 Josh. 3. 7–end Matt. 10. 1–22	Prov. 25. 6–14 Ps. 33. 6–12 Eph. 4. 1–6 G Luke 14. 1–11	Ps. 123; 124 Isa. 49. 13–23 Luke 12. 1–12	Ps. 125; 126 Josh. 3. 7–end Matt. 10. 1–22
Ps. *72*; 75 Ecclus. 6. 14–end *or* Ezek. 10. 1–19 Mark 14. 1–11 Gr	**Denys, Bishop of Paris, Martyr, *c.* 250** Com. Martyr	1 Kings ch. 21 Acts 21.37 – 22.21	Ecclus. 6. 14–end *or* Ezek. 10. 1–19 Mark 14. 1–11
Ps. 74 Ecclus. 7. 27–end *or* Ezek. 11. 14–end Mark 14. 12–25 G		1 Kings 22. 1–28 Acts 22.22 – 23.11	Ecclus. 7. 27–end *or* Ezek. 11. 14–end Mark 14. 12–25
Ps. 119. 81–104 Ecclus. 10. 6–8, 12–24 *or* Ezek. 12. 1–16 Mark 14. 26–42 G		1 Kings 22. 29–45 Acts 23. 12–end	Ecclus. 10. 6–8, 12–24 *or* Ezek. 12. 1–16 Mark 14. 26–42
Ps. 78. 40–end† Ecclus. 11. 7–28 *or* Ezek. 12. 17–end Mark 14. 43–52 G		2 Kings 1. 2–17 Acts 24. 1–23	Ecclus. 11. 7–28 *or* Ezek. 12. 17–end Mark 14. 43–52
Ps. 69 Ecclus. 14.20 – 15.10 *or* Ezek. 13. 1–16 Mark 14. 53–65 Gw	**Edward the Confessor, King of England, 1066, translated 1163** Com. Saint	2 Kings 2. 1–18 Acts 24.24 – 25.12	Ecclus. 14.20 – 15.10 *or* Ezek. 13. 1–16 Mark 14. 53–65

October 2006

		Sunday Principal Service Weekday Eucharist	Third Service Morning Prayer
14	Sa	Gal. 3. 22–end Ps. 105. 1–7 Luke 11. 27–28	Ps. 76; 79 2 Kings 4. 1–37 Acts 25. 13–end
	G		

15 S **THE EIGHTEENTH SUNDAY AFTER TRINITY (Proper 23)**

		Track 1	*Track 2*	
15	S	Job 23. 1–9, 16–end Ps. 22. 1–15 Heb. 4. 12–end	Amos 5. 6–7, 10–15 Ps. 90. 12–end Heb. 4. 12–end	Ps. 129; 130 Isa. 50. 4–10 Luke 13. 22–30
	G	Mark 10. 17–31	Mark 10. 17–31	

16 M *Nicholas Ridley, Bishop of London, and Hugh Latimer, Bishop of Worcester, Reformation Martyrs, 1555*

16 DEL 28	M	Gal. 4. 21–24, 26–27, 31; 5. 1 Ps. 113 Luke 11. 29–32	Ps. 80; 82 2 Kings ch. 5 Acts 26. 1–23
	G		

17 Tu **Ignatius, Bishop of Antioch, Martyr, c. 107**

17	Tu	Com. Martyr *also* Phil. 3. 7–12 John 6. 52–58	*or* Gal. 5. 1–6 Ps. 119. 41–48 Luke 11. 37–41	Ps. 87; 89. *1–18* 2 Kings 6. 1–23 Acts 26. 24–end
	Gr			

18 W **LUKE THE EVANGELIST**

18	W	Isa. 35. 3–6 *or* Acts 16. 6–12a Ps. 147. 1–7 2 Tim. 4. 5–17 Luke 10. 1–9	*MP:* Ps. 145; 146 Isa. ch. 55 Luke 1. 1–4
	R		

19 Th **Henry Martyn, Translator of the Scriptures, Missionary in India and Persia, 1812**

19	Th	Com. Missionary *esp.* Mark 16. 15–end *also* Isa. 55. 6–11	*or* Eph. 1. 1, 3–10 Ps. 98. 1–4 Luke 11. 47–end	Ps. 90; *92* 2 Kings 9. 17–end Acts 27. 27–end
	Gw			

20	F	Eph. 1. 11–14 Ps. 33. 1–6, 12 Luke 12. 1–7	Ps. *88* (95) 2 Kings 12. 1–9 Acts 28. 1–16
	G		
21	Sa	Eph. 1. 15–end Ps. 8 Luke 12. 8–12	Ps. 96; *97*; 100 2 Kings 17. 1–23 Acts 28. 17–end
	G		

22 S **THE NINETEENTH SUNDAY AFTER TRINITY (Proper 24)**

		Track 1	*Track 2*	
22	S	Job 38. 1–7 [34–end] Ps. 104. 1–10 [26, 35c] Heb. 5. 1–10	Isa. 53. 4–end Ps. 91. 9–end Heb. 5. 1–10	Ps. 133; 134; 137. 1–6 Isa. 54. 1–14 Luke 13. 31–end
	G	Mark 10. 35–45	Mark 10. 35–45	

23 DEL 29	M	Eph. 2. 1–10 Ps. 100 Luke 12. 13–21	Ps. *98*; 99; 101 2 Kings 17. 24–end Phil. 1. 1–11
	G		
24	Tu	Eph. 2. 12–end Ps. 85. 7–end Luke 12. 35–38	Ps. *106*† (*or* 103) 2 Kings 18. 1–12 Phil. 1. 12–end
	G		

Second Service Evening Prayer	Calendar and Holy Communion	Morning Prayer	Evening Prayer
Ps. 81; *84* Ecclus. 15. 11–end *or* Ezek. 14. 1–11 Mark 14. 66–end **ct**	G	2 Kings 4. 1–37 Acts 25. 13–end	Ecclus. 15. 11–end *or* Ezek. 14. 1–11 Mark 14. 66–end **ct**
	THE EIGHTEENTH SUNDAY AFTER TRINITY		
Ps. 127 [128] Josh. 5.13 – 6.20 Matt. 11. 20–end	Deut. 6. 4–9 Ps. 122 1 Cor. 1. 4–8 G Matt. 22. 34–end	Ps. 129; 130 Isa. 50. 4–10 Luke 13. 22–30	Ps. 127; [128] Josh. 5.13 – 6.20 Matt. 11. 20–end
Ps. *85*; 86 Ecclus. 16. 17–end *or* Ezek. 14. 12–end Mark 15. 1–15	G	2 Kings ch. 5 Acts 26. 1–23	Ecclus. 16. 17–end *or* Ezek. 14. 12–end Mark 15. 1–15
Ps. 89. 19–end Ecclus. 17. 1–24 *or* Ezek. 18. 1–20 Mark 15. 16–32 *or First EP of Luke* Ps. 33 Hos. 6. 1–3 2 Tim. 3. 10–end **R ct**	**Etheldreda, Abbess of Ely, 679** Com. Abbess Gw	2 Kings 6. 1–23 Acts 26. 24–end	Ecclus. 17. 1–24 *or* Ezek. 18. 1–20 Mark 15. 16–32 *or First EP of Luke* (Ps. 33) Hos. 6. 1–3 2 Tim. 3. 10–end **R ct**
EP: Ps. 103 Ecclus. 38. 1–14 *or* Isa. 61. 1–6 Col. 4. 7–end	**LUKE THE EVANGELIST** Isa. 35. 3–6 Ps. 147. 1–6 2 Tim. 4. 5–15 Luke 10. 1–9 R *or* Luke 7. 36–50	(Ps. 145; 146) Isa. ch. 55 Luke 1. 1–4	(Ps. 103) Ecclus. 38. 1–14 *or* Isa. 61. 1–6 Col. 4. 7–end
Ps. 94 Ecclus. 19. 4–17 *or* Ezek. 20. 1–20 Mark 15. 42–end	G	2 Kings 9. 17–end Acts 27. 27–end	Ecclus. 19. 4–17 *or* Ezek. 20. 1–20 Mark 15. 42–end
Ps. 102 Ecclus. 19. 20–end *or* Ezek. 20. 21–38 Mark 16. 1–8	G	2 Kings 12. 1–9 Acts 28. 1–16	Ecclus. 19. 20–end *or* Ezek. 20. 21–38 Mark 16. 1–8
Ps. 104 Ecclus. 21. 1–17 *or* Ezek. 24. 15–end Mark 16. 9–end **ct**	G	2 Kings 17. 1–23 Acts 28. 17–end	Ecclus. 21. 1–17 *or* Ezek. 24. 15–end Mark 16. 9–end **ct**
	THE NINETEENTH SUNDAY AFTER TRINITY		
Ps. 141 Josh. 14. 6–14 Matt. 12. 1–21	Gen. 18. 23–32 Ps. 141. 1–9 Eph. 4. 17–end G Matt. 9. 1–8	Ps. 133; 134; 137. 1–6 Isa. 54. 1–14 Luke 13. 31–end	Ps. 142 Josh. 14. 6–14 Matt. 12. 1–21
Ps. *105*† (*or* 103) Ecclus. 22. 6–22 *or* Ezek. 28. 1–19 John 13. 1–11	G	2 Kings 17. 24–end Phil. 1. 1–11	Ecclus. 22. 6–22 *or* Ezek. 28. 1–19 John 13. 1–11
Ps. 107† Ecclus. 22.27 – 23.15 *or* Ezek. 33. 1–20 John 13. 12–20	G	2 Kings 18. 1–12 Phil. 1. 12–end	Ecclus. 22.27 – 23.15 *or* Ezek. 33. 1–20 John 13. 12–20

October 2006

	Sunday Principal Service / Weekday Eucharist	Third Service / Morning Prayer

25 W

Crispin and Crispinian, Martyrs at Rome, c. 287

Eph. 3. 2–12
Ps. 98
Luke 12. 39–48

110; *111*; 112
2 Kings 18. 13–end
Phil. 2. 1–13

G

---

26 Th

Alfred the Great, King of the West Saxons, Scholar, 899
Cedd, Abbot of Lastingham, Bishop of the East Saxons, 664*
Com. Saint   *or* Eph. 3. 14–end
also 2 Sam. 23. 1–5   Ps. 33. 1–6
John 18. 33–37   Luke 12. 49–53

Ps. 113; *115*
2 Kings 19. 1–19
Phil. 2. 14–end

Gw

---

27 F

Eph. 4. 1–6
Ps. 24. 1–6
Luke 12. 54–end

Ps. 139
2 Kings 19. 20–36
Phil. 3.1 – 4.1

G

---

28 Sa

SIMON AND JUDE, APOSTLES

Isa. 28. 14–16
Ps. 119. 89–96
Eph. 2. 19–end
John 15. 17–27

MP: Ps. 116; 117
Wisd. 5. 1–16
or Isa. 45. 18–end
Luke 6. 12–16

R

---

29 S

THE LAST SUNDAY AFTER TRINITY (Proper 25)**

Track 1   *Track 2*
Job 42. 1–6, 10–end   Jer. 31. 7–9
Ps. 34. 1–8 [19–end]   Ps. 126
Heb. 7. 23–end   Heb. 7. 23–end
Mark 10. 46–end   Mark 10. 46–end

G

Ps. 119. 89–104
Isa. 59. 9–20
Luke 14. 1–14

or, if being observed as Bible
Sunday:

Isa. 55. 1–11
Ps. 19. 7–end
2 Tim. 3.14 – 4.5
John 5. 36b–end

G

Ps. 119. 89–104
Isa. 45. 22–end
Matt. 24. 30–35
or Luke 14. 1–14

---

30 M
DEL 30

Eph. 4.32 – 5.8
Ps. 1
Luke 13. 10–17

Ps. 123; 124; 125; *126*
2 Kings 21. 1–18
1 Tim. 1. 1–17

G

---

31 Tu

Martin Luther, Reformer, 1546

Eph. 5. 21–end
Ps. 128
Luke 13. 18–21

Ps. *132*; 133
2 Kings 22.1 – 23.3
1 Tim. 1.18 – 2.end

G

---

*Chad may be celebrated with Cedd on 26 October instead of 2 March.
**If the Dedication Festival is kept on this Sunday, use the provision given on 30 September and 1 October.

Second Service Evening Prayer	Calendar and Holy Communion	Morning Prayer	Evening Prayer
Ps. 119. 129–152 Ecclus. 24. 1–22 *or* Ezek. 33. 21–end John 13. 21–30	**Crispin, Martyr at Rome, *c.* 287** Com. Martyr Gr	2 Kings 18. 13–end Phil. 2. 1–13	Ecclus. 24. 1–22 *or* Ezek. 33. 21–end John 13. 21–30
Ps. 114; *116*; 117 Ecclus. 24. 23–end *or* Ezek. 34. 1–16 John 13. 31–end	G	2 Kings 19. 1–19 Phil. 2. 14–end	Ecclus. 24. 23–end *or* Ezek. 34. 1–16 John 13. 31–end
Ps. *130*; 131; 137 Ecclus. 27.30 – 28.9 *or* Ezek. 34. 17–end John 14. 1–14 *or First EP of Simon and Jude* Ps. 124; 125; 126 Deut. 32. 1–4 John 14. 15–26 **R ct**	G	2 Kings 19. 20–36 Phil. 3.1 – 4.1	Ecclus. 27.30 – 28.9 *or* Ezek. 34. 17–end John 14. 1–14 *or First EP of Simon and Jude* (Ps. 124; 125; 126) Deut. 32. 1–4 John 14. 15–26 **R ct**
EP: Ps. 119. 1–16 1 Macc. 2. 42–66 *or* Jer. 3. 11–18 Jude 1–4, 17–25	**SIMON AND JUDE, APOSTLES** Isa. 28. 9–16 Ps. 116. 11–end Jude 1–8 *or* Rev. 21. 9–14 John 15. 17–end R	(Ps. 119. 89–96) Wisd. 5. 1–16 *or* Isa. 45. 18–end Luke 6. 12–16	(Ps. 119. 1–16) 1 Macc. 2. 42–66 *or* Jer. 3. 11–18 Eph. 2. 19–end
	THE TWENTIETH SUNDAY AFTER TRINITY		
Ps. 119. 121–136 Eccles. chs. 11 and 12 2 Tim. 2. 1–7 *Gospel:* Luke 18. 9–14	Prov. 9. 1–6 Ps. 145. 15–end Eph. 5. 15–21 Matt. 22. 1–14	Ps. 119. 89–104 Isa. 59. 9–20 Luke 14. 1–14	Ps. 119. 121–136 Eccles. chs. 11 and 12 2 Tim. 2. 1–7
Ps. 119. 1–16 2 Kings ch. 22 Col. 3. 12–17 *Gospel:* Luke 4. 14–30	G		
Ps. *127*; 128; 129 Ecclus. 31. 1–11 *or* Ezek. 37. 1–14 John 15. 1–11	G	2 Kings 21. 1–18 1 Tim. 1. 1–17	Ecclus. 31. 1–11 *or* Ezek. 37. 1–14 John 15. 1–11
First EP of All Saints Ps. 1; 5 Ecclus. 44. 1–15 *or* Isa. 40. 27–31 Rev. 19. 6–10 **W ct** *or, if All Saints is observed on 5th:* Ps. (134); *135* Ecclus. 34. 9–end *or* Ezek. 37. 15–end John 15. 12–17		2 Kings 22.1 – 23.3 1 Tim. 1.18 – 2.end	*First EP of All Saints* Ps. 1; 5 Ecclus. 44. 1–15 *or* Isa. 40. 27–31 Rev. 19. 6–10 **W ct**

November 2006

			Sunday Principal Service / **Weekday Eucharist**	**Third Service** / **Morning Prayer**

1 W — **ALL SAINTS' DAY**

	Sunday Principal Service / Weekday Eucharist	Third Service / Morning Prayer
♄	Wisd. 3. 1–9 *or* Isa. 25. 6–9 Ps. 24. 1–6 Rev. 21. 1–6a John 11. 32–44	*MP*: Ps. 15; 84; 149 Isa. 35. 1–9 Luke 9. 18–27
♄	*or, if the readings above are used on Sunday 5 November:* Isa. 56. 3–8 *or* 2 Esdras 2. 42–end Ps. 33. 1–5 Heb. 12. 18–24 Matt. 5. 1–12	*MP*: Ps. 111; 112; 117 Wisd. 5. 1–16 *or* Jer. 31. 31–34 2 Cor. 4. 5–12
G	*or, if kept as a feria:* Eph. 6. 1–9 Ps. 145. 10–20 Luke 13. 22–30	Ps. 119. 153–end 2 Kings 23. 4–25 1 Tim. ch. 3

2 Th — **Commemoration of the Faithful Departed (All Souls' Day)**

	Sunday Principal Service / Weekday Eucharist		Third Service / Morning Prayer
	Lam. 3. 17–26, 31–33 *or* Wisd. 3. 1–9 Ps. 23 *or* Ps. 27. 1–6, 16–end Rom. 5. 5–11 *or* 1 Pet. 1. 3–9	*or* Eph. 6. 10–20 Ps. 144. 1–2, 9–11 Luke 13. 31–end	Ps. *143*; 146 2 Kings. 23.36 – 24.17 1 Tim. ch. 4
Rp *or*	*or* John 5. 19–25		
Gp	*or* John 6. 37–40		

3 F — **Richard Hooker, Priest, Anglican Apologist, Teacher, 1600**
Martin of Porres, Friar, 1639

	Sunday Principal Service / Weekday Eucharist		Third Service / Morning Prayer
	Com. Teacher *esp.* John 16. 12–15	*or* Phil. 1. 1–11 Ps. 111 Luke 14. 1–6	Ps. 142; *144* 2 Kings 24.18 – 25.12
Rw *or*	*also* Ecclus. 44. 10–15		1 Tim. 5. 1–16
Gw			

4 Sa

	Sunday Principal Service / Weekday Eucharist	Third Service / Morning Prayer
	Phil. 1. 18–26 Ps. 42. 1–7 Luke 14. 1, 7–11	Ps. 147 2 Kings 25. 22–end 1 Tim. 5. 17–end
R *or* **G**		

5 S — THE FOURTH SUNDAY BEFORE ADVENT

	Sunday Principal Service / Weekday Eucharist	Third Service / Morning Prayer
	Deut. 6. 1–9 Ps. 119. 1–8 Heb. 9. 11–14 Mark 12. 28–34	Ps. 112; 149 Jer. 31. 31–34 1 John 3. 1–3
R *or* **G**		
♄	*Or ALL SAINTS' SUNDAY (see readings for 1 November throughout the day)*	

6 M — *Leonard, Hermit, 6th century; William Temple, Archbishop of Canterbury, Teacher, 1944*

DEL 31

	Sunday Principal Service / Weekday Eucharist	Third Service / Morning Prayer
	Phil. 2. 1–4 Ps. 131 Luke 14. 12–14	Ps. 2; 146 *alt.* Ps. *1*; 2; 3 Dan. ch. 1 Rev. ch. 1
R *or* **G**		

7 Tu — **Willibrord of York, Bishop, Apostle of Fresia, 739**

	Sunday Principal Service / Weekday Eucharist		Third Service / Morning Prayer
	Com. Missionary *esp.* Isa. 52. 7–10	*or* Phil. 2. 5–11 Ps. 22. 22–27 Luke 14. 15–24	Ps. *5*; 147. 1–12 *alt.* Ps. *5*; 6; (8) Dan. 2. 1–24
Rw *or*	Matt. 28. 16–end		Rev. 2. 1–11
Gw			

8 W — **The Saints and Martyrs of England**

	Sunday Principal Service / Weekday Eucharist	Third Service / Morning Prayer
	Isa. 61. 4–9 *or* Ecclus. 44. 1–15 Ps. 15	Phil. 2. 12–18 Ps. 27. 1–5 Luke 14. 25–33	Ps. *9*; 147. 13–end *alt.* Ps. 119. 1–32 Dan. 2. 25–end Rev. 2. 12–end
Rw *or*	Rev. 19. 5–10	
Gw	John 17. 18–23	

9 Th — *Margery Kempe, Mystic, c. 1440*

	Sunday Principal Service / Weekday Eucharist	Third Service / Morning Prayer
	Phil. 3. 3–8 Ps. 105. 1–7 Luke 15. 1–10	Ps. 11; *15*; 148 *alt.* Ps. 14; *15*; 16 Dan. 3. 1–18 Rev. 3. 1–13
R *or* **G**		

Second Service Evening Prayer		Calendar and Holy Communion	Morning Prayer	Evening Prayer
EP: Ps. 148; 150 Isa. 65. 17–end Heb. 11.32 – 12.2		**ALL SAINTS' DAY** Isa. 66. 20–23 Ps. 33. 1–5 Rev. 7. 2–4[5–8]9–12 Matt. 5. 1–12	Ps. 15; 84; 149 Isa. 35. 1–9 Luke 9. 18–27	Ps. 148; 150 Isa. 65. 17–end Heb. 11.32 – 12.2
EP: Ps. 145 Isa. 66. 20–23 Col. 1. 9–14				
Ps. 136 Ecclus. ch. 35 *or* Ezek. 39. 21–end John 15. 18–end	ℬ			
Ps. *138*; 140; 141 Ecclus. 37. 7–24 *or* Ezek. 43. 1–12 John 16. 1–15		To celebrate All Souls' Day, see *Common Worship* provision. 2 Kings. 23.36 – 24.17 1 Tim. ch. 4	Ecclus. 37. 7–24 *or* Ezek. 43. 1–12 John 16. 1–15
	G			
Ps. 145 Ecclus. 38. 1–14 *or* Ezek. 44. 4–16 John 16. 16–22	G		2 Kings 24.18 – 25.12 1 Tim. 5. 1–16	Ecclus. 38. 1–14 *or* Ezek. 44. 4–16 John 16. 16–22
Ps. *148*; 149; 150 Ecclus. 38. 24–end *or* Ezek. 47. 1–12 John 16. 23–end ct	G		2 Kings 25. 22–end 1 Tim. 5. 17–end	Ecclus. 38. 24–end *or* Ezek. 47. 1–12 John 16. 23–end ct
Ps. 145. 1–9 [10–end] Dan. 2. 1–11 [12–24] 25–48 Rev. 7. 9–end *Gospel:* Matt. 5. 1–12	G	**THE TWENTY-FIRST SUNDAY AFTER TRINITY** Gen. 32. 24–29 Ps. 90. 1–12 Eph. 6. 10–20 John 4. 46b–end	Ps. 112; 149 Jer. 31. 31–34 1 John 3. 1–3	Ps. 145. 1–9 [10–end] Dan. 2. 1–11 [12–24] 25–48 Rev. 7. 9–end
Ps. *92*; 96; 97 *alt.* Ps. *4*; 7 Isa. 1. 1–20 Matt. 1. 18–end	Gw	**Leonard, Hermit, 6th century** Com. Abbot	Dan. ch. 1 Rev. ch. 1	Isa. 1. 1–20 Matt. 1. 18–end
Ps. 98; 99; *100* *alt.* Ps. *9*; 10† Isa. 1. 21–end Matt. 2. 1–15	G		Dan. 2. 1–24 Rev. 2. 1–11	Isa. 1. 21–end Matt. 2. 1–15
Ps. 111; *112*; 116 *alt.* Ps. *11*; 12; 13 Isa. 2. 1–11 Matt. 2. 16–end	G		Dan. 2. 25–end Rev. 2. 12–end	Isa. 2. 1–11 Matt. 2. 16–end
Ps. 118 *alt.* Ps. 18† Isa. 2. 12–end Matt. ch. 3	G		Dan. 3. 1–18 Rev. 3. 1–13	Isa. 2. 12–end Matt. ch. 3

November 2006

	Sunday Principal Service Weekday Eucharist	Third Service Morning Prayer

10 F **Leo the Great, Bishop of Rome, Teacher, 461**
Com. Teacher   *or* Phil. 3.17 – 4.1
also 1 Pet. 5. 1–11   Ps. 122
Rw *or*   Luke 16. 1–8
Gw

Ps. *16*; 149
alt. Ps. 17; *19*
Dan. 3. 19–end
Rev. 3. 14–end

---

11 Sa **Martin, Bishop of Tours, *c.* 397**
Com. Bishop   *or* Phil. 4. 10–19
also 1 Thess. 5. 1–11   Ps. 112
Matt. 25. 34–40   Luke 16. 9–15
Rw *or*
Gw

Ps. *16*; 149
alt. Ps. 20; 21; *23*
Dan. 4. 1–18
Rev. ch. 4

---

12 S THE THIRD SUNDAY BEFORE ADVENT
(Remembrance Sunday)

Jonah 3. 1–5, 10
Ps. 62. 5–end
Heb. 9. 24–end
G *or* **R**   Mark 1. 14–20

Ps. 136
Mic. 4. 1–5
Phil. 4. 6–9

---

13 M **Charles Simeon, Priest, Evangelical Divine, 1836**
DEL 32   Com. Pastor   *or* Titus 1. 1–9
esp. Mal. 2. 5–7   Ps. 24. 1–6
Rw *or* *also* Col. 1. 3–8   Luke 17. 1–6
Gw Luke 8. 4–8

Ps. 19; *20*
alt. Ps. 27; *30*
Dan. 4. 19–end
Rev. ch. 5

---

14 Tu *Samuel Seabury, first Anglican Bishop in North America, 1796*
Titus 2. 1–8, 11–14
Ps. 37. 3–5, 30–32
Luke 17. 7–10
R *or* **G**

Ps. *21*; 24
alt. Ps. 32; *36*
Dan. 5. 1–12
Rev. ch. 6

---

15 W
Titus 3. 1–7
Ps. 23
Luke 17. 11–19
R *or* **G**

Ps. *23*; 25
alt. Ps. 34
Dan. 5. 13–end
Rev. 7. 1–4, 9–end

---

16 Th **Margaret, Queen of Scotland, Philanthropist, Reformer of the Church, 1093**
Edmund Rich of Abingdon, Archbishop of Canterbury, 1240
Com. Saint   *or* Philemon 7–20
also Prov. 31. 10–12, 20,   Ps. 146. 4–end
26–end   Luke 17. 20–25
Rw *or* 1 Cor. 12.13 – 13.3
Gw Matt. 25. 34–end

Ps.*26*; 27
alt. Ps. 37†
Dan. ch. 6
Rev. ch. 8

---

17 F **Hugh, Bishop of Lincoln, 1200**
Com. Bishop   *or* 2 John 4–9
also 1 Tim. 6. 11–16   Ps. 119. 1–8
Rw *or*   Luke 17. 26–end
Gw

Ps. 28; *32*
alt. Ps. 31
Dan. 7. 1–14
Rev. 9. 1–12

---

18 Sa **Elizabeth of Hungary, Princess of Thuringia, Philanthropist, 1231**
Com. Saint   *or* 3 John 5–8
esp. Matt. 25. 31–end   Ps. 112
also Prov. 31. 10–end   Luke 18. 1–8
Rw *or*
Gw

Ps. 33
alt. Ps. 41; *42*; 43
Dan. 7. 15–end
Rev. 9. 13–end

---

19 S THE SECOND SUNDAY BEFORE ADVENT
Dan. 12. 1–3
Ps. 16
Heb. 10. 1–14 [15–18] 19–25
R *or* **G**   Mark 13. 1–8

Ps. 96
1 Sam. 9.27 – 10.2a; 10. 17–26
Matt. 13. 31–35

---

20 M **Edmund, King of the East Angles, Martyr, 870**
DEL 33   *Priscilla Lydia Sellon, a Restorer of the Religious Life in the Church of England, 1876*
Com. Martyr   *or* Rev. 1. 1–4; 2. 1–5
also Prov. 20. 28; 21. 1–4, 7   Ps. 1
R *or* **Gr**   Luke 18. 35–end

Ps.*46*; *47*
alt. Ps. 44
Dan. 8. 1–14
Rev. ch. 10

Second Service Evening Prayer		Calendar and Holy Communion	Morning Prayer	Evening Prayer
Ps. 137; 138; *143* *alt.* Ps. 22 Isa. 3. 1–15 Matt. 4. 1–11	G		Dan. 3. 19–end Rev. 3. 14–end	Isa. 3. 1–15 Matt. 4. 1–11
Ps. 145 *alt.* Ps. 24; *25* Isa. 4.2 – 5.7 Matt. 4. 12–22 ct	Gw	**Martin, Bishop of Tours, *c.* 397** Com. Bishop	Dan. 4. 1–18 Rev. ch. 4	Isa. 4.2 – 5.7 Matt. 4. 12–22 ct
		THE TWENTY-SECOND SUNDAY AFTER TRINITY		
Ps. 46 [82] Isa. 10.33 – 11.9 John 14. [1–22] 23–29		Gen. 45. 1–7, 15 Ps. 133 Phil. 1. 3–11 Matt. 18. 21–end	Ps. 136 Mic. 4. 1–5 Phil. 4. 6–9	Ps. 144 Isa. 10.33 – 11.9 John 14. [1–22] 23–29
Ps. 34 *alt.* Ps. 26; *28*; 29 Isa. 5. 8–24 Matt. 4.23 – 5.12	Gw	**Britius, Bishop of Tours, 444** Com. Bishop	Dan. 4. 19–end Rev. ch. 5	Isa. 5. 8–24 Matt. 4.23 – 5.12
Ps. 36; *40* *alt.* Ps. 33 Isa. 5. 25–end Matt. 5. 13–20	G	Dan. 5. 1–12	Isa. 5. 25–end Rev. ch. 6	Matt. 5. 13–20
Ps. 37 *alt.* Ps. 119. 33–56 Isa. ch. 6 Matt. 5. 21–37	Gw	**Machutus, Bishop, Apostle of Brittany, *c.* 564** Com. Bishop	Dan. 5. 13–end Rev. 7. 1–4, 9–end	Isa. ch. 6 Matt. 5. 21–37
Ps. 42; *43* *alt.* Ps. 39; *40* Isa. 7. 1–17 Matt. 5. 38–end	G		Dan. ch. 6 Rev. ch. 8	Isa. 7. 1–17 Matt. 5. 38–end
Ps. 31 *alt.*Ps. 35 Isa. 8. 1–15 Matt. 6. 1–18	Gw	**Hugh, Bishop of Lincoln, 1200** Com. Bishop	Dan. 7. 1–14 Rev. 9. 1–12	Isa. 8. 1–15 Matt. 6. 1–18
Ps. 84; *86* *alt.* Ps. 45; *46* Isa. 8.16 – 9.7 Matt. 6. 19–end ct	G		Dan. 7. 15–end Rev. 9. 13–end	Isa. 8.16 – 9.7 Matt. 6. 19–end ct
Ps. 95 Dan. 3. [1–12] 13–end Matt. 13. 24–30, 36–43	G	**THE TWENTY-THIRD SUNDAY AFTER TRINITY** Isa. 11. 1–10 Ps. 44. 1–9 Phil. 3. 17–end Matt. 22. 15–22	Ps. 96 1 Sam. 9.27 – 10.2a; 10. 17–26 Matt. 13. 31–35	Ps. 95 Dan. 3. [1–12] 13–end Matt. 13. 24–30, 36–43
Ps. 70; *71* *alt.* Ps. *47*; 49 Isa. 9.8 – 10.4 Matt. 7. 1–12	Gr	**Edmund, King of the East Angles, Martyr, 870** Com. Martyr	Dan. 8. 1–14 Rev. ch. 10	Isa. 9.8 – 10.4 Matt. 7. 1–12

November 2006

	Sunday Principal Service / Weekday Eucharist	Third Service / Morning Prayer

21 Tu
R or G

Rev. 3. 1–6, 14–end
Ps. 15
Luke 19. 1–10

Ps. 48; *52*
alt. Ps. *48*; 52
Dan. 8. 15–end
Rev. 11. 1–14

22 W   *Cecilia, Martyr at Rome, c. 230*
R or G

Rev. ch. 4
Ps. 150
Luke 19. 11–28

Ps. *56*; 57
alt. Ps. 119. 57–80
Dan. 9. 1–19
Rev. 11. 15–end

23 Th   **Clement, Bishop of Rome, Martyr, *c.* 100**
Com. Martyr   *or*   Rev. 5. 1–10
also Phil. 3.17 – 4.3   Ps. 149. 1–5
Matt. 16. 13–19   Luke 19. 41–44
R or Gr

Ps. 61; *62*
alt. Ps. 56; *57*; (63†)
Dan. 9. 20–end
Rev. ch. 12

24 F
R or G

Rev. 10. 8–11
Ps. 119. 65–72
Luke 19. 45–end

Ps. *63*; 65
alt. Ps. *51*; 54
Dan. 10.1 – 11.1
Rev. 13. 1–10

25 Sa   *Catherine of Alexandria, Martyr, 4th century; Isaac Watts, Hymn Writer, 1748*

Rev. 11. 4–12
Ps. 144. 1–9
Luke 20. 27–40

Ps. 78. 1–39
alt. Ps. 68
Dan. ch. 12
Rev. 13. 11–end

R or G

26 S   CHRIST THE KING
The Sunday Next Before Advent
R or W

Dan. 7. 9–10, 13–14
Ps. 93
Rev. 1. 4b–8
John 18. 33–37

MP: Ps. 29; 110
Isa. 32. 1–8
Rev. 3. 7–end

27 M
DEL 34
R or G

Rev. 14. 1–5
Ps. 24. 1–6
Luke 21. 1–4

Ps. 92; *96*
alt. Ps. 71
Isa. 40. 1–11
Rev. 14. 1–13

28 Tu
R or G

Rev. 14. 14–19
Ps. 96
Luke 21. 5–11

Ps. *97*; 98; 100
alt. Ps. 73
Isa. 40. 12–26
Rev. 14.15 – 15.end

29 W

Rev. 15. 1–4
Ps. 98
Luke 21. 12–19

Ps. 110; 111; *112*
alt. Ps. 77
Isa. 40.27 – 41.7
Rev. 16. 1–11

R or G

G   *Day of Intercession and Thanksgiving for the Missionary Work of the Church*

Isa. 49. 1–6; Isa. 52. 7–10; Mic. 4. 1–5
Acts 17. 12–end; 2 Cor. 5.14 – 6.2; Eph. 2. 13–end
Ps. 2; 46; 47
Matt. 5. 13–16; Matt. 28. 16–end; John 17. 20–end

Second Service Evening Prayer	Calendar and Holy Communion	Morning Prayer	Evening Prayer
Ps. *67*; 72 *alt.* Ps. 50 Isa. 10. 5–19 Matt. 7. 13–end **G**		Dan. 8. 15–end Rev. 11. 1–14	Isa. 10. 5–19 Matt. 7. 13–end
Ps. 73 *alt.* Ps. *59*; 60 (67) Isa. 10. 20–32 Matt. 8. 1–13 **Gr**	**Cecilia, Martyr at Rome, *c*. 230** Com. Virgin Martyr	Dan. 9. 1–19 Rev. 11. 15–end	Isa. 10. 20–32 Matt. 8. 1–13
Ps. 74; *76* *alt.* Ps. 61; *62*; 64 Isa. 10.33 – 11.9 Matt. 8. 14–22 **Gr**	**Clement, Bishop of Rome, Martyr, *c*. 100** Com. Martyr	Dan. 9. 20–end Rev. ch. 12	Isa. 10.33 – 11.9 Matt. 8. 14–22
Ps. 77 *alt.* Ps. 38 Isa. 11.10 – 12.end Matt. 8. 23–end **G**		Dan. 10.1 – 11.1 Rev. 13. 1–10	Isa. 11.10 – 12.end Matt. 8. 23–end
78. 40–end *alt.* Ps. 65; *66* Isa. 13. 1–13 Matt. 9. 1–17 **ct** *or First EP of Christ the King* Ps. 99; 100 Isa. 10.33 – 11.9 1 Tim. 6. 11–16 **R** *or* **W ct**	**Catherine of Alexandria, Martyr, 4th century** Com. Virgin Martyr **Gr**	Dan. ch. 12 Rev. 13. 11–end	Isa. 13. 1–13 Matt. 9. 1–17 **ct**
EP: Ps. 72. 1–7 [8–end] Dan. ch. 5 John 6. 1–15	**THE SUNDAY NEXT BEFORE ADVENT** To celebrate Christ the King, see *Common Worship* provision. Jer. 23. 5–8 Ps. 85. 8–end Col. 1. 13–20 **G** John 6. 5–14	Ps. 29; 110 Isa. 32. 1–8 Rev. 3. 7–end	Ps. 72. 1–7 [8–end] Dan. ch. 5 Rev. 1. 4b–8
Ps. *80*; 81 *alt.* Ps. *72*; 75 Isa. 14. 3–20 Matt. 9. 18–34 **G**		Isa. 40. 1–11 Rev. 14. 1–13	Isa. 14. 3–20 Matt. 9. 18–34
Ps. 99; *101* *alt.* Ps. 74 Isa. ch. 17 Matt. 9.35 – 10.15 **G**		Isa. 40. 12–26 Rev. 14.15 – 15.end	Isa. ch. 17 Matt. 9.35 – 10.15
Ps. 121; *122*; 123; 124 *alt.* Ps. 119. 81–104 Isa. ch. 19 Matt. 10. 16–33 *or First EP of Andrew the Apostle* Ps. 48 Isa. 49. 1–9a 1 Cor. 4. 9–16 **R ct**		Isa. 40.27 – 41.7 Rev. 16. 1–11	Isa. ch. 19 Matt. 10. 16–33 *or First EP of Andrew the Apostle* (Ps. 48) Isa. 49. 1–9a 1 Cor. 4. 9–16 **R ct**
	To celebrate the Day of Intercession and Thanksgiving for the Missionary Work of the Church, see *Common Worship* provision. **G**		

November 2006

	Sunday Principal Service Weekday Eucharist	Third Service Morning Prayer

30 Th R	ANDREW THE APOSTLE	Isa. 52. 7–10 Ps. 19. 1–6 Rom. 10. 12–18 Matt. 4. 18–22	*MP:* Ps. 47; 147. 1–12 Ezek. 47. 1–12 *or* Ecclus. 14. 20–end John 12. 20–32

December 2006

		Sunday Principal Service Weekday Eucharist	Third Service Morning Prayer
1 F R *or* G	*Charles de Foucauld, Hermit in the Sahara, 1916*	Rev. 20.1–4, 11 – 21.2 Ps. 84. 1–6 Luke 21. 29–33	Ps. 139 *alt.* Ps. 55 Isa. 41.21 – 42.9 Rev. ch. 17
2 Sa R *or* G		Rev. 22. 1–7 Ps. 95. 1–7 Luke 21. 34–36	Ps. 145 *alt.* Ps. 76; 79 Isa. 42. 10–17 Rev. ch. 18
3 S P	THE FIRST SUNDAY OF ADVENT CW Year C begins	Jer. 33. 14–16 Ps. 25. 1–10 1 Thess. 3. 9–end Luke 21. 25–36	Ps. 44 Isa. 51. 4–11 Rom. 13. 11–end
4 M P	*John of Damascus, Monk, Teacher, c. 749; Nicholas Ferrar, Deacon, Founder of the Little Gidding Community, 1637* Daily Eucharistic Lectionary Year 1 begins	Isa. 2. 1–5a Ps. 122 Matt. 8. 5–11	Ps. 50; 54 *alt.* Ps. 1; 2; 3 Isa. 42. 18–end Rev. ch. 19
5 Tu P		Isa. 11. 1–10 Ps. 72. 1–4, 18–19 Luke 10. 21–24	Ps. 80; 82 *alt.* Ps. 5; 6; (8) Isa. 43. 1–13 Rev. ch. 20
6 W Pw	Nicholas, Bishop of Myra, *c.* 326 Com. Bishop *or* *also* Isa. 61. 1–3 1 Tim. 6. 6–11 Mark 10. 13–16	Isa. 25. 6–10a Ps. 23 Matt. 15. 29–37	Ps. 5; 7 *alt.* Ps. 119. 1–32 Isa. 43. 14–end Rev. 21. 1–8
7 Th Pw	Ambrose, Bishop of Milan, Teacher, 397 Com. Teacher *or* *also* Isa. 41. 9b–13 Luke 22. 24–30	Isa. 26. 1–6 Ps. 118. 18–27a Matt. 7. 21, 24–27	Ps. 42; 43 *alt.* Ps. 14; 15; 16 Isa. 44. 1–8 Rev. 21. 9–21
8 F Pw	The Conception of the Blessed Virgin Mary Com. BVM *or*	Isa. 29. 17–end Ps. 27. 1–4, 16–17 Matt. 9. 27–31	Ps. 25; 26 *alt.* Ps. 17; 19 Isa. 44. 9–23 Rev. 21.22 – 22.5
9 Sa P		Isa. 30. 19–21, 23–26 Ps. 146. 4–9 Matt. 9.35 – 10.1, 6–8	Ps. 9; (10) *alt.* Ps. 20; 21; 23 Isa. 44.24 – 45.13 Rev. 22. 6–end
10 S P	THE SECOND SUNDAY OF ADVENT	Baruch 5. 1–9 *or* Mal. 3. 1–4 *Canticle:* Benedictus Phil. 1. 3–11 Luke 3. 1–6	Ps. 80 Isa. 64. 1–7 Matt. 11. 2–11

Second Service Evening Prayer		Calendar and Holy Communion	Morning Prayer	Evening Prayer
EP: Ps. 87; 96 Zech. 8. 20–end John 1. 35–42	R	**ANDREW THE APOSTLE** Zech. 8. 20–end Ps. 92. 1–5 Rom. 10. 9–end Matt. 4. 18–22	(Ps. 47; 147. 1–12) Ezek. 47. 1–12 *or* Ecclus. 14. 20–end John 12. 20–32	(Ps. 87; 96) Isa. 52. 7–10 John 1. 35–42
Ps. *146*; 147 *alt.* Ps. 69 Isa. 22. 1–14 Matt. 11. 2–19	G		Isa. 41.21 – 42.9 Rev. ch. 17	Isa. 22. 1–14 Matt. 11. 2–19
Ps. 148; 149; *150* *alt.* Ps. 81; *84* Isa. ch. 24 Matt. 11. 20–end	G		Isa. 42. 10–17 Rev. ch. 18	Isa. ch. 24 Matt. 11. 20–end
Ps. 9. 1–8 [9–end] Joel 3. 9–end Rev. 14.13 – 15.4 *Gospel:* John 3. 1–17	P	**THE FIRST SUNDAY IN ADVENT** Advent 1 Collect until Christmas Eve Mic. 4. 1–4, 6–7 Ps. 25. 1–9 Rom. 13. 8–14 Matt. 21. 1–13	Ps. 44 Isa. 51. 4–11 Rom. 13. 11–end	Ps. 9. 1–8 [9–end] Joel 3. 9–end Rev. 14.13 – 15.4
Ps. 70; *71* *alt.* Ps. *4*; 7 Isa. 25. 1–9 Matt. 12. 1–21	P		Isa. 42. 18–end Rev. ch. 19	Isa. 25. 1–9 Matt. 12. 1–21
Ps. *74*; 75 *alt. 9*; 10† Isa. 26. 1–13 Matt. 12. 22–37	P		Isa. 43. 1–13 Rev. ch. 20	Isa. 26. 1–13 Matt. 12. 22–37
Ps. 76; 77 *alt.* Ps. *11*; 12; 13 Isa. 28. 1–13 Matt. 12. 38–end	Pw	**Nicholas, Bishop of Myra, *c.* 326** Com. Bishop	Isa. 43. 14–end Rev. 21. 1–8	Isa. 28. 1–13 Matt. 12. 38–end
Ps. *40*; 46† *alt.* Ps. 18† Isa. 28. 14–end Matt. 13. 1–23	P		Isa. 44. 1–8 Rev. 21. 9–21	Isa. 28. 14–end Matt. 13. 1–23
Ps. 16; *17* *alt.* Ps. 22 Isa. 29. 1–14 Matt. 13. 24–43	Pw	**The Conception of the Blessed Virgin Mary** Isa. 44. 9–23 Rev. 21.22 – 22.5		Isa. 29. 1–14 Matt. 13. 24–43
Ps. 27; *28* *alt.* Ps. *24*; 25 Isa. 29. 15–end Matt. 13. 44–end ct	P		Isa. 44.24 – 45.13 Rev. 22. 6–end	Isa. 29. 15–end Matt. 13. 44–end ct
Ps. 75 [76] Isa. 40. 1–11 Luke 1. 1–25	P	**THE SECOND SUNDAY IN ADVENT** 2 Kings 22. 8–10; 23. 1–3 Ps. 50. 1–6 Rom. 15. 4–13 Luke 21. 25–33	Ps. 40 Isa. 64. 1–7 Luke 3. 1–6	Ps. 75 [76] Mal. 3. 1–4 Luke 1. 1–25

December 2006

		Sunday Principal Service Weekday Eucharist	Third Service Morning Prayer
11 M P		Isa. ch. 35 Ps. 85. 7–end Luke 5. 17–26	Ps. 44 *alt.* Ps. 27; *30* Isa. 45. 14–end 1 Thess. ch. 1
12 Tu P		Isa. 40. 1–11 Ps. 96. 1, 10–end Matt. 18. 12–14	Ps. *56*; 57 *alt.* Ps. 32; *36* Isa. ch. 46 1 Thess. 2. 1–12
13 W Pr	**Lucy, Martyr at Syracuse, 304** Ember Day* *Samuel Johnson, Moralist, 1784* Com. Martyr *or* *also* Wisd. 3. 1–7 2 Cor. 4. 6–15	 Isa. 40. 25–end Ps. 103. 8–13 Matt. 11. 28–end	 Ps. *62*; 63 *alt.* Ps. 34 Isa. ch. 47 1 Thess. 2. 13–end
14 Th Pw	**John of the Cross, Poet, Teacher, 1591** Com. Teacher *or* *esp.* 1 Cor. 2. 1–10 *also* John 14. 18–23	 Isa. 41. 13–20 Ps. 145. 1, 8–13 Matt. 11. 11–15	Ps. 53; *54*; 60 *alt.* Ps. 37† Isa. 48. 1–11 1 Thess. ch. 3
15 F P	Ember Day*	Isa. 48. 17–19 Ps. 1 Matt. 11. 16–19	Ps. 85; *86* *alt.* Ps. 31 Isa. 48. 12–end 1 Thess. 4. 1–12
16 Sa P	Ember Day*	Ecclus. 48. 1–4, 9–11 *or* 2 Kings 2. 9–12 Ps. 80. 1–4, 18–19 Matt. 17. 10–13	Ps. 145 *alt.* Ps. 41; *42*; 43 Isa. 49. 1–13 1 Thess. 4. 13–end
17 S P	THE THIRD SUNDAY OF ADVENT O Sapientia	 Zeph. 3. 14–end *Canticle:* Isa. 12. 2–6 *or* Ps. 146. 4–end Phil. 4. 4–7 Luke 3. 7–18	 Ps. 12; 14 Isa. 25. 1–9 1 Cor. 4. 1–5
18 M P		Jer. 23. 5–8 Ps. 72. 1–2, 12–13, 18–end Matt. 1. 18–24	Ps. 40 *alt.* Ps. 44 Isa. 49. 14–25 1 Thess. 5. 1–11
19 Tu P		Judg. 13. 2–7, 24–end Ps. 71. 3–8 Luke 1. 5–25	Ps. 144; *146* Isa. ch. 50 1 Thess. 5. 12–end
20 W P		Isa. 7. 10–14 Ps. 24. 1–6 Luke 1. 26–38	Ps. 46; 95 Isa. 51. 1–8 2 Thess. ch. 1
21 Th** P		Zeph. 3. 14–18 Ps. 33. 1–4, 11–12, 19–end Luke 1. 39–45	Ps. *121*; 122; 123 Isa. 51. 9–16 2 Thess. ch. 2

*For Ember Day provision, see p. 13.
**Thomas the Apostle may be celebrated on 21 December instead of 3 July.

Second Service Evening Prayer	Calendar and Holy Communion	Morning Prayer	Evening Prayer
Ps. *144*; 146 *alt.* Ps. 26; *28*; 29 Isa. 30. 1–18 Matt. 14. 1–12		Isa. 45. 14–end 1 Thess. ch. 1	Isa. 30. 1–18 Matt. 14. 1–12
	P		
Ps. *11*; 12; 13 *alt.* Ps. 33 Isa. 30. 19–end Matt. 14. 13–end		Isa. ch. 46 1 Thess. 2. 1–12	Isa. 30. 19–end Matt. 14. 13–end
	P		
	Lucy, Martyr at Syracuse, 304 Com. Virgin Martyr		
Ps. *10*; 14 *alt.* Ps. 119. 33–56 Isa. ch. 31 Matt. 15. 1–20		Isa. ch. 47 1 Thess. 2. 13–end	Isa. ch. 31 Matt. 15. 1–20
	Pr		
Ps. 73 *alt.* Ps. 39; *40* Isa. ch. 32 Matt. 15. 21–28		Isa. 48. 1–11 1 Thess. ch. 3	Isa. ch. 32 Matt. 15. 21–28
	P		
Ps. 82; *90* *alt.* Ps. 35 Isa. 33. 1–22 Matt. 15. 29–end		Isa. 48. 12–end 1 Thess. 4. 1–12	Isa. 33. 1–22 Matt. 15. 29–end
	P		
Ps. 93; *94* *alt.* Ps. 45; *46* Isa. ch. 35 Matt. 16. 1–12 ct	**O Sapientia**	Isa. 49. 1–13 1 Thess. 4. 13–end	Isa. ch. 35 Matt. 16. 1–12
	P		ct
	THE THIRD SUNDAY IN ADVENT Isa. 35. 1–10 Ps. 80. 1–7 1 Cor. 4. 1–5 Matt. 11. 2–10	Ps. 12; 14 Isa. 25. 1–9 Luke 3. 7–18	Ps. 62 Zeph. 3. 14–end Luke 1. 57–66 [67–end]
Ps. 50. 1–6; [62] Isa. ch. 35 Luke 1. 57–66 [67–end]	P		
Ps. 25; *26* *alt.* Ps. *47*; 49 Isa. 38. 1–8, 21–22 Matt. 16. 13–end		Isa. 49. 14–25 1 Thess. 5. 1–11	Isa. 38. 1–8, 21–22 Matt. 16. 13–end
	P		
Ps. 10; *57* Isa. 38. 9–20 Matt. 17. 1–13		Isa. ch. 50 1 Thess. 5. 12–end	Isa. 38. 9–20 Matt. 17. 1–13
	P		
Ps. *4*; 9 Isa. ch. 39 Matt. 17. 14–21	Ember Day Ember CEG	Isa. 51. 1–8 2 Thess. ch. 1	Isa. ch. 39 Matt. 17. 14–21 *or First EP of Thomas the Apostle* (Ps. 27) Isa. ch. 35 Heb. 10.35 – 11.1 **R ct**
	P		
Ps. 80; *84* Zeph. 1.1 – 2.3 Matt. 17. 22–end	**THOMAS THE APOSTLE** Job 42. 1–6 Ps. 139. 1–11 Eph. 2. 19–end	(Ps. 92; 146) 2 Sam. 15. 17–21 *or* Ecclus. ch. 2	(Ps. 139) Hab. 2. 1–4 1 Pet. 1. 3–12
	R John 20. 24–end	John 11. 1–16	

December 2006

		Sunday Principal Service Weekday Eucharist	Third Service Morning Prayer
22	F	1 Sam. 1. 24–end Ps. 113 Luke 1. 46–56	Ps. *124*; 125; 126; 127 Isa. 51. 17–end 2 Thess. ch. 3
	P		
23	Sa	Mal. 3. 1–4; 4. 5–end Ps. 25. 3–9 Luke 1. 57–66	Ps. 128; 129; *130*; 131 Isa. 52. 1–12 Jude
	P		

24   S

THE FOURTH SUNDAY OF ADVENT
CHRISTMAS EVE

	Mic. 5. 2–5a *Canticle:* Magnificat *or* Ps. 80. 1–8 Heb. 10. 5–10 Luke 1. 39–45 [46–55]	Ps. 144 Isa. 32. 1–8 Rev. 22. 6–end

P

25   M

CHRISTMAS DAY

| *Any of the following sets of readings may be used on the evening of Christmas Eve and on Christmas Day. Set III should be used at some service during the celebration.* | *I*
Isa. 9. 2–7
Ps. 96
Titus 2. 11–14
Luke 2. 1–14 [15–20]
II
Isa. 62. 6–end
Ps. 97
Titus 3. 4–7
Luke 2. [1–7] 8–20
III
Isa. 52. 7–10
Ps. 98
Heb. 1. 1–4 [5–12]
John 1. 1–14 | *MP:* Ps. *110*; 117
Isa. 62. 1–5
Matt. 1. 18–end |

℣

26   Tu

STEPHEN, DEACON, FIRST MARTYR

| *The reading from Acts must be used as either the first or second reading at the Eucharist.* | 2 Chron. 24. 20–22
or Acts 7. 51–end
Ps. 119. 161–168
Acts 7. 51–60
or Gal. 2. 16b–20
Matt. 10. 17–22 | *MP:* Ps. *13*; 31. 1–8; 150
Jer. 26. 12–15
Acts ch. 6 |

R

27   W

JOHN, APOSTLE AND EVANGELIST

	Exod. 33. 7–11a Ps. 117 1 John ch. 1 John 21. 19b–end	*MP:* Ps. *21*; 147. 13–end Exod. 33. 12–end 1 John 2. 1–11

W

28   Th

THE HOLY INNOCENTS

	Jer. 31. 15–17 Ps. 124 1 Cor. 1. 26–29 Matt. 2. 13–18	*MP:* Ps. *36*; 146 Baruch 4. 21–27 *or* Gen. 37. 13–20 Matt. 18. 1–10

R

29   F
      Wr

Thomas Becket, Archbishop of Canterbury, Martyr, 1170*

Com. Martyr *esp.* Matt. 10. 28–33 *also* Ecclus. 51. 1–8	*or* 1 John 2. 3–11 Ps. 96. 1–4 Luke 2. 22–35	Ps. *19*; 20 Isa. 57. 15–end John 1. 1–18

*Thomas Becket may be celebrated on 7 July instead of 29 December.

Second Service Evening Prayer		Calendar and Holy Communion	Morning Prayer	Evening Prayer
Ps. 24; *48* Zeph. 3. 1–13 Matt. 18. 1–20	**P**	Ember Day Ember CEG	Isa. 51. 17–end 2 Thess. ch. 3	Zeph. 3. 1–13 Matt. 18. 1–20
Ps. 89. 1–37 Zeph. 3. 14–end Matt. 18. 21–end **ct**	**P**	Ember Day Ember CEG	Isa. 52. 1–12 Jude	Zeph. 3. 14–end Matt. 18. 21–end **ct**
Evening Prayer Ps. 85 Zech. ch. 2 Rev. 1. 1–8	**P**	**THE FOURTH SUNDAY IN ADVENT** **CHRISTMAS EVE** Isa. 40. 1–9 Ps. 145. 17–end Phil. 4. 4–7 John 1. 19–28	Ps. 144 Isa. 32. 1–8 Rev. 22. 6–end	Ps. 85 Zech. ch. 2 Rev. 1. 1–8
EP: Ps. 8 Isa. 65. 17–25 Phil. 2. 5–11 *or* Luke 2. 1–20 *if it has not been used at the Principal Service of the day*	**ꟸ**	**CHRISTMAS DAY** Isa. 9. 2–7 Ps. 98 Heb. 1. 1–12 John 1. 1–14	Ps. 110; 117 Isa. 62. 1–5 Matt. 1. 18–end	Ps. 8 Isa. 65. 17–25 Phil. 2. 5–11 *or* Luke 2. 1–20
EP: Ps. 57; *86* Gen. 4. 1–10 Matt. 23. 34–end	**R**	**STEPHEN, DEACON, FIRST MARTYR** Collect (1) Stephen (2) Christmas 2 Chron. 24. 20–22 Ps. 119. 161–168 Acts 7. 55–end Matt. 23. 34–end	(Ps. 13; 31. 1–8; 150) Jer. 26. 12–15 Acts ch. 6	(Ps. 57; 86) Gen. 4. 1–10 Matt. 10. 17–22
EP: Ps. 97 Isa. 6. 1–8 1 John 5. 1–12	**W**	**JOHN, APOSTLE AND EVANGELIST** Collect (1) John (2) Christmas Exod. 33. 18–end Ps. 92. 11–end 1 John ch. 1 John 21. 19b–end	(Ps. 21; 147. 13–end) Exod. 33. 7–11a 1 John 2. 1–11	(Ps. 97) Isa. 6. 1–8 1 John 5. 1–12
EP: Ps. 123; *128* Isa. 49. 14–25 Mark 10. 13–16	**R**	**THE HOLY INNOCENTS** Collect (1) Innocents (2) Christmas Jer. 31. 10–17 Ps. 123 Rev. 14. 1–5 Matt. 2. 13–18	(Ps. 36; 146) Baruch 4. 21–27 *or* Gen. 37. 13–20 Matt. 18. 1–10	(Ps. 123; *128*) Isa. 49. 14–25 Mark 10. 13–16
Ps. 131; *132* Jonah ch. 1 Col. 1. 1–14	**W**	**CEG of Christmas**	Isa. 57. 15–end John 1. 1–18	Jonah ch. 1 Col. 1. 1–14

December 2006

	Sunday Principal Service Weekday Eucharist	Third Service Morning Prayer

30 Sa

	1 John 2. 12–17	Ps. 111; 112; *113*
	Ps. 96. 7–10	Isa. 59. 1–15a
W	Luke 2. 36–40	John 1. 19–28

31 S   THE FIRST SUNDAY OF CHRISTMAS

	1 Sam. 2. 18–20, 26	Ps. 105. 1–11
	Ps. 148. 1–6[7–end]	Isa. 41.21 – 42.1
	Col. 3. 12–17	1 John 1. 1–7
W	Luke 2. 41–end	

Second Service Evening Prayer	Calendar and Holy Communion	Morning Prayer	Evening Prayer
	CEG of Christmas		
Ps. *65*; 84		Isa. 59. 1–15a	Jonah ch. 2
Jonah ch. 2			
Col. 1. 15–23		John 1. 19–28	Col. 1. 15–23
ct	W		ct
	THE FIRST SUNDAY OF CHRISTMAS		
Ps. 132	Isa. 62. 10–12	Ps. 105. 1–11	Ps. 132
Isa. ch. 61	Ps. 45. 1–7	Isa. 41.21 – 42.1	Isa. ch. 61
Gal. 3.27 – 4.7	Gal. 4. 1–7	1 John 1. 1–7	Luke 2. 15–21
or Luke 2. 15–21	W Matt. 1. 18–end		

CALENDAR 2006

JANUARY

Su	X^1	B	E^2	E^3	E^4	.	.
M	2	9	16	23	30	.	.
Tu	3	10	17	24	31	.	.
W	4	11	18	25	.	.	.
Th	5	12	19	26	.	.	.
F	E	13	20	27	.	.	.
Sa	7	14	21	28	.	.	.

FEBRUARY

Su	.	.	L^{-4}	L^{-3}	L^{-2}	L^{-1}	.
M	.	.	6	13	20	27	.
Tu	.	.	7	14	21	28	.
W	1	8	15	22	.	.	.
Th	Pr	9	16	23	.	.	.
F	3	10	17	24	.	.	.
Sa	4	11	18	25	.	.	.

MARCH

Su	.	.	L^1	L^2	L^3	L^4	.
M	.	.	6	13	20	27	.
Tu	.	.	7	14	21	28	.
W	A	8	15	22	29	.	.
Th	2	9	16	23	30	.	.
F	3	10	17	24	31	.	.
Sa	4	11	18	An	.	.	.

APRIL

Su	.	.	L^5	P	E	E^2	E^3
M	.	.	3	10	17	24	.
Tu	.	.	4	11	18	25	.
W	.	.	5	12	19	26	.
Th	.	.	E	M	20	27	.
F	.	.	7	G	21	28	.
Sa	1	8	15	22	29	.	.

MAY

Su	.	.	E^4	E^5	E^6	E^7	.
M	1	8	15	22	29	.	.
Tu	2	9	16	23	30	.	.
W	3	10	17	24	31	.	.
Th	4	11	18	A	.	.	.
F	5	12	19	26	.	.	.
Sa	6	13	20	27	.	.	.

JUNE

Su	.	.	W	T	T^1	T^2	.
M	.	.	5	12	19	26	.
Tu	.	.	6	13	20	27	.
W	.	.	7	14	21	28	.
Th	1	8	15	22	29	.	.
F	2	9	16	23	30	.	.
Sa	3	10	17	24	.	.	.

JULY

Su	.	.	T^3	T^4	T^5	T^6	T^7
M	.	.	3	10	17	24	31
Tu	.	.	4	11	18	25	.
W	.	.	5	12	19	26	.
Th	.	.	6	13	20	27	.
F	.	.	7	14	21	28	.
Sa	1	8	15	22	29	.	.

AUGUST

Su	.	.	T^8	T^9	T^{10}	T^{11}	.
M	.	.	7	14	21	28	.
Tu	1	8	15	22	29	.	.
W	2	9	16	23	30	.	.
Th	3	10	17	24	31	.	.
F	4	11	18	25	.	.	.
Sa	5	12	19	26	.	.	.

SEPTEMBER

Su	.	T^{12}	T^{13}	T^{14}	T^{15}	.	.
M	.	.	4	11	18	25	.
Tu	.	.	5	12	19	26	.
W	.	.	6	13	20	27	.
Th	.	.	7	14	21	28	.
F	1	8	15	22	29	.	.
Sa	2	9	16	23	30	.	.

OCTOBER

Su	T^{16}	T^{17}	T^{18}	T^{19}	T^L	.	.
M	2	9	16	23	30	.	.
Tu	3	10	17	24	31	.	.
W	4	11	18	25	.	.	.
Th	5	12	19	26	.	.	.
F	6	13	20	27	.	.	.
Sa	7	14	21	28	.	.	.

NOVEMBER

Su	.	.	A^{-4}	A^{-3}	A^{-2}	A^{-1}	.
M	.	.	6	13	20	27	.
Tu	.	.	7	14	21	28	.
W	AS	8	15	22	29	.	.
Th	2	9	16	23	30	.	.
F	3	10	17	24	.	.	.
Sa	4	11	18	25	.	.	.

DECEMBER

Su	.	.	A^1	A^2	A^3	A^4	X^1
M	.	.	4	11	18	X	.
Tu	.	.	5	12	19	26	.
W	.	.	6	13	20	27	.
Th	.	.	7	14	21	28	.
F	1	8	15	22	29	.	.
Sa	2	9	16	23	30	.	.

A = Ash Wednesday, Ascension, Advent	E = Epiphany, Easter	T = Trinity
A^- = Before Advent	E^4 = also Presentation (if trans.)	(T^8 = also Transfiguration, 2006)
A^{-1} = Christ the King	G = Good Friday	T^L = Last Sunday after Trinity
A^{-4} = also All Saints (if trans.)	L = Lent	W = Pentecost (Whit Sunday)
An = Annunciation	L^- = Before Lent	X = Christmas
AS = All Saints	M = Maundy Thursday	
B = Baptism	P = Palm Sunday	
	Pr = Presentation	

CALENDAR 2007

	JANUARY						
Su	. .	B	E^2	E^3	E^4	. .	
M	1	8	15	22	29	. .	
Tu	2	9	16	23	30	. .	
W	3	10	17	24	31	. .	
Th	4	11	18	25	. .	. .	
F	5	12	19	26	. .	. .	
Sa	E	13	20	27	. .	. .	

	FEBRUARY					
Su	. .	L^{-3}	L^{-2}	L^{-1}	L^1	. .
M	. .	5	12	19	26	. .
Tu	. .	6	13	20	27	. .
W	. .	7	14	A	28	. .
Th	1	8	15	22	. .	. .
F	Pr	9	16	23	. .	. .
Sa	3	10	17	24	. .	. .

	MARCH					
Su	. .	L^2	L^3	L^4	L^5	. .
M	. .	5	12	19	An	. .
Tu	. .	6	13	20	27	. .
W	. .	7	14	21	28	. .
Th	1	8	15	22	29	. .
F	2	9	16	23	30	. .
Sa	3	10	17	24	31	. .

	APRIL					
Su	P	E	E^2	E^3	E^4	. .
M	2	9	16	23	30	. .
Tu	3	10	17	24	. .	. .
W	4	11	18	25	. .	. .
Th	M	12	19	26	. .	. .
F	G	13	20	27	. .	. .
Sa	7	14	21	28	. .	. .

	MAY					
Su	. .	E^5	E^6	E^7	W	. .
M	. .	7	14	21	28	. .
Tu	1	8	15	22	29	. .
W	2	9	16	23	30	. .
Th	3	10	A	24	31	. .
F	4	11	18	25	. .	. .
Sa	5	12	19	26	. .	. .

	JUNE					
Su	. .	T	T^1	T^2	T^3	. .
M	. .	4	11	18	25	. .
Tu	. .	5	12	19	26	. .
W	. .	6	13	20	27	. .
Th	. .	7	14	21	28	. .
F	1	8	15	22	29	. .
Sa	2	9	16	23	30	. .

	JULY					
Su	T^4	T^5	T^6	T^7	T^8	. .
M	2	9	16	23	30	. .
Tu	3	10	17	24	31	. .
W	4	11	18	25	. .	. .
Th	5	12	19	26	. .	. .
F	6	13	20	27	. .	. .
Sa	7	14	21	28	. .	. .

	AUGUST					
Su	. .	T^9	T^{10}	T^{11}	T^{12}	. .
M	. .	6	13	20	27	. .
Tu	. .	7	14	21	28	. .
W	1	8	15	22	29	. .
Th	2	9	16	23	30	. .
F	3	10	17	24	31	. .
Sa	4	11	18	25	. .	. .

	SEPTEMBER					
Su	. .	T^{13}	T^{14}	T^{15}	T^{16}	T^{17}
M	. .	3	10	17	24	. .
Tu	. .	4	11	18	25	. .
W	. .	5	12	19	26	. .
Th	. .	6	13	20	27	. .
F	. .	7	14	21	28	. .
Sa	1	8	15	22	29	. .

	OCTOBER					
Su	. .	T^{18}	T^{19}	T^{20}	T^L	. .
M	1	8	15	22	29	. .
Tu	2	9	16	23	30	. .
W	3	10	17	24	31	. .
Th	4	11	18	25	. .	. .
F	5	12	19	26	. .	. .
Sa	6	13	20	27	. .	. .

	NOVEMBER					
Su	. .	A^{-4}	A^{-3}	A^{-2}	A^{-1}	. .
M	. .	5	12	19	26	. .
Tu	. .	6	13	20	27	. .
W	. .	7	14	21	28	. .
Th	AS	8	15	22	29	. .
F	2	9	16	23	30	. .
Sa	3	10	17	24	. .	. .

	DECEMBER					
Su	. .	A^1	A^2	A^3	A^4	X^1
M	. .	3	10	17	24	31
Tu	. .	4	11	18	X	. .
W	. .	5	12	19	26	. .
Th	. .	6	13	20	27	. .
F	. .	7	14	21	28	. .
Sa	1	8	15	22	29	. .

A = Ash Wednesday, Ascension, Advent	E^4 = also Presentation (if trans.)	(T^3 = also Birth of John the Baptist, 2007)
A^- = Before Advent	G = Good Friday	(T^7 = also Mary Magdalene, 2007)
A^{-1} = Christ the King	L = Lent	T^L = Last Sunday after Trinity
A^{-4} = also All Saints (if trans.)	L^- = Before Lent	(T^L = also Simon and Jude, 2007)
An = Annunciation	M = Maundy Thursday	W = Pentecost (Whit Sunday)
AS = All Saints	P = Palm Sunday	X = Christmas
B = Baptism	Pr = Presentation	
E = Epiphany, Easter	T = Trinity